# MEMOIRS OF A MODERN SCOTLAND

# Memoirs of a Modern Scotland

edited by
KARL MILLER

FABER AND FABER
London

*First published in 1970*
*by Faber and Faber Limited*
*24 Russell Square London WC1*
*Printed in Great Britain by*
*Latimer Trend & Co Ltd Plymouth*
*All rights reserved*

SBN 571 08750 7

# Contents

CONTENTS

8

# Illustrations

9

# Preface

These essays and memoirs are published in honour of Hector
MacIver, who was born on the island of Lewis in the Hebrides
on 3 August 1910 and who died at Temple, Midlothian, on
30 April 1966. He went to school in the Hebrides, studied at
Edinburgh University, and became a teacher. During the war
he served in the Navy. He was a writer, a broadcaster, a talker,
a speaker, and he produced plays. He was a gifted man, and a
gifted friend. Some of those who knew him decided to write
about him, and to write about him in the context of an account,
by themselves and others, of the times he lived in. The contributors include people who live in Scotland and people who
do not; they include the Gaelic poet, Sorley MacLean, who was
Hector MacIver's friend over many years, and Louis Simpson,
a fine American poet, who never knew him, but who has taken
an interest in Scottish literature and has written a book on
James Hogg. Outsiders—foreigners and expatriates, Americans
especially—have in the past had something to say about Scottish literature. This, perhaps, is to state the invidious—since
several of the present company are outsiders. Living in London,
I am one myself, and I have felt presumptuous in expressing
opinions here about Scotland. We can claim, however, that
others in the same situation have done so too.

The collection offers a description of some of the things that
were happening in literature and the arts in Scotland during
Hector MacIver's adult years. His own life was one of these
things; it deserves to be described. He was not famous in the
usual sense, but he made contributions to more than one of the
fields under discussion and he did have a kind of fame. It went

by word of mouth and seldom reached the newspapers; it was as oral as the world of his origins. He was like a byword or a ballad. I hope we haven't spoiled the Ballad of Hector MacIver—as James Hogg's mother told Walter Scott that he had spoiled the Minstrelsy of the Scottish Border—by writing it down.

The essays are largely about a time that is past, about the modern Scotland which began after the First World War and lasted out the Second. The main tracks followed in the essays are the course of Modernism itself; what might be called the romantic survival; and the progress of Scottish Nationalism. One of their less predictable features is the prominence which it was thought necessary to give to the activities of poets— during a period when poetry has seemed to many in Britain to be of declining importance, the most doubtful of the arts. It is true that in recent decades poets have been found less than before in London, and have often preferred to remain, or to settle, far away from the south of England, but there is more to it than that. In Scotland it has been the leading poets—Hugh MacDiarmid and Edwin Muir—who have played the leading part in divining and projecting, both in their verse and their prose, the significant dramas and anxieties of these years. These are the Scottish writers who have mattered most.

Other poets too, in Scotland, have seen what many have been incapable of seeing. The poets who write here about the threatened societies that survive in the depopulated north and north-west, Sorley MacLean and George Mackay Brown, both refer, with an inwardness that is striking, to atomic warfare: they are like men who have already experienced some of its devastations. Few except poets have been able to see such meanings in the life of their communities. Few communities have been able to yield such meanings.

Acknowledgments are due to the *Listener*, where passages of Arthur Marwick's essay, Hugh MacDiarmid's piece on Lang-holm, and part of Stuart Hood's essay, first appeared; to the *New Statesman*, where I published Muriel Spark's 'What Images Return'; and to the *New Left Review*, where sections of Tom Nairn's essay first appeared. I want to thank Robert Taubman, Hector MacIver's early pupil, Charles McAra, his colleague, and Alastair Reid, for their help in preparing the book. It was Robert Regan, one of Hector's captains during the war, whose idea it was that a book of this sort might be done. He has suffered patiently delays in execution which were altogether remote from the traditions of the service.

# 1

## Scottish Nationalism since 1918

### by Arthur Marwick

In studying any political movement it is always important to bear in mind the distinctions between those who found and lead a specific organisation, those who form its rank-and-file membership and those who, from time to time, vote for or otherwise identify with it. The political structure of Great Britain is so ordered that the endeavours of any minor party must always seem either absurd or, if at all successful, a trifle sinister. Yet there is nothing absurd or sinister about the basic sentiment to which Scottish Nationalism makes its appeal. Scotsmen do feel a pride in being Scots, do sometimes feel irritated by the alien manners and assumptions of the English. A government at Westminster based on a parliament in which English members have an overwhelming majority inevitably gives English interests precedence over Scottish whenever the two are in conflict. When faced with the standard argument about the need to sink national differences in a greater internationalism, Scottish Nationalists can plausibly retort that there is nothing specially internationalist about the dominance of a small power by a bigger one. The sympathetic Englishman wonders what all the fuss is about; the other type of Englishman, whose opinions are expressed in classic form in the opening pages of Mr A. J. P. Taylor's *English History 1914–1945* (Professor Medlicott more recently has published his *Contemporary England*—only the Scots and the Americans, it seems, write about 20th-century *Britain*), doesn't even know that there is a fuss. The point to be made at the outset is that in all the claims of Scottish Nationalism there is a certain irreducible minimum of clear common sense and rational sentiment. In the past, politicians of progressive outlook almost by definition favoured some form of self-

13

government for Scotland: that was the position of the Liberals, of the ILP, of Willie Gallacher, the only Communist to hold a Parliamentary seat for more than a few months, and of the Labour Party till 1945. The problem for the nationalist organisations has been to persuade ordinary Scotsmen that the claims of nationalism should take precedence over the other preoccupations and loyalties of our age, preoccupations with social welfare or social status, loyalties to class, group, trade union, or to one of the British political parties.

Modern nationalism in Scotland is made up of two basic ingredients, one best described by the essentially 19th-century term, 'Home Rule', and the other nationalist in the fullest sense of the term. Home Rulers stressed administrative efficiency, decentralisation, and the supreme virtue of self-government as an abstract ideal: their aim was a local Scottish parliament within a federal United Kingdom. The mainspring of nationalism proper is the deep and real fear that Scotland as a separate nation, with a distinct and valuable cultural tradition, is doomed to extinction through emigration and the invasion of alien values, unless she resumes complete control of her own affairs. In practice the two ingredients have been mixed in a pretty dense solution, though on the whole the history of Scottish Nationalism in the 20th century is of the disintegration of the Home Rule ingredient and the precipitation of the nationalist one. The persistence of the Gladstonian element can be seen in the explanation offered by the Scottish Nationalist Party in 1953 of why, when the EIIR cypher was so objectionable, feelings had not similarly been ruffled over the title of Edward VII:

> Railways, banks and most industrial concerns were under Scottish control. Scottish business ran its own investment policy. Local authorities were masters of their own affairs. There was free trade. The only important controls reserved in London were over central taxes, foreign affairs and defence.

The first phase of the modern nationalist resurgence is linked to the patriotic stirrings of World War I and to the severe economic depression which followed that war. The second is related to the rather different emotions aroused by the Second World War and to the hostility evoked by the centralising policies of the 1940s: lasting from around 1942 till the early Fifties,

14

it saw something of a re-emphasis on the older Home Rule tradition. The third phase, insistently nationalist again, began some time in 1962; we are still in its thrall.

It is fairly easy to determine what sorts and conditions of men have formed the activists in the movement, less easy to be sure about the rank-and-file and about the voters. The professions are well-represented (if England is a nation of shopkeepers, Scotland is a nation of actuaries and notaries)—especially those with a vested Scottish interest: lawyers obviously, since Scots law remains distinct from, but constantly encroached upon by, English law; but also local government officials who object to the whittling of local authority powers as embodied, above all, in the hotly contested Local Government Act of 1929; doctors who feel grievances against centralised medical services; and teachers who feel threatened by government educational policies. Poets and men from the Scottish bohemia have always been prominent, though not always welcome: theirs has been ¥ the genuine cause of a literary tradition in danger. Students, too, have been much in evidence, especially students from Glasgow University which, more than any other, has provided that point of contact between Lowland and Highland civilisation which is in itself a potent generator of the sparks of national sentiment. The clerical class, traditional home everywhere of extreme nationalism, has played an important part in the Scottish movement. Expatriates seem to have been specially susceptible to the appeal of nationalism: Arthur Donaldson, present party leader, was just beginning his successful career in American business when he joined the original Nationalist Party of Scotland in 1928. The movement has proudly brandished the lairds, the landed and titled gentlemen, who have been associated with it. To hazard a generalisation, it seems that the leadership, at least, has been largely drawn from those who fall outside normal group affiliations—such as trade unions—or from those who find themselves involved in a clear Scottish affiliation which can be set against a relevant English or British one: for example, Scots law and English law, Scottish peerage and British peerage. To say all this is inevitably to create an image of a determinedly right-wing movement. Yet any such image would be completely false: many leading Nationalists have been avowed socialists, and the Scottish

15

Nationalist Party today proudly declares its policy to be 'slightly left of centre'. Clearly there can be no consistent social ideology in a party which puts nationalism first: in general, the political party which the Scottish Nationalists have touched most closely at most points is, not surprisingly, the Liberal Party—and it is in regard to the Liberals that the problems of electoral strategy have been most acute.

The first phase of modern nationalism arose on the ashes of the old Liberal programme of Home Rule All Round, destroyed utterly by the untoward turn of events in Ireland at the end of the First World War. The energetic puffing of Scottish socialists who entered the House of Commons in the Twenties produced a modest afterglow, but none of the Home Rule Bills introduced by George Buchanan (an ILP member, closely associated with Jimmie Maxton), or later by James Barr (also a member of the ILP, but essentially a Labour loyalist), got beyond a second reading. Outside Parliament a somewhat sporadic propaganda was kept up by the Scottish Home Rule Association—whose leading light was Roland Muirhead, who in his early years had distinguished himself by walking out of the family business to go and live in an Owenite colony in the state of Washington, USA—upholders of the Gladstonian ideal; by the Scottish National Movement—leading light, the poet and journalist, Lewis Spence, immaculate always in bowler hat and spats—which was primarily orientated towards the restoration and preservation of Scottish literary traditions; by the Scots National League, which through its important monthly, *Scots Independent*, preached complete separation from England— leading figure, Tom Gibson, a lawyers' clerk, who later became secretary of the British Steel Federation; and by the Glasgow University Scottish Nationalist Association, the creation of J. M. MacCormick, a law student with, at that time, links of a superficial sort with the Scottish ILP. In April 1928 the four bodies merged to form the Nationalist Party of Scotland, whose declared objective was 'to secure self-government for Scotland with independent national status within the British group of nations'. An inauguration demonstration, held on the anniversary of Bannockburn (23 June) near the site of the battle, followed. Since such 'tartan tories' as the Duke of Montrose held aloof from the new party, later (1933) joining with dissident

16

members of the Cathcart (Glasgow) Unionist party to form the
Scottish Party, men of the Left predominated. C. M. Grieve (the
poet, Hugh MacDiarmid) explained his presence on the
platform:

> I have been 20 years a member of the ILP and an active
> socialist worker but I am of opinion that the position and
> prospects of Scotland today are so deplorable and ineffective,
> and action in regard thereto on the part of the overwhelm-
> ingly English legislature so impossible that it behoves all true
> Scots of whatever party to sink their other differences in the
> meantime in the interest of the great national reconstruction
> movement.

Before the year's end the new party had plunged into two
rather different electoral campaigns: at Glasgow University the
president of the party, R. B. Cunninghame Graham, a figure of
high romance who had associations both with Keir Hardie and
with South America, was narrowly defeated by Stanley Baldwin
for the rectorship; but in the party's first by-election Lewis
Spence came bottom of the poll, presumably little assisted by
his eve-of-the-poll address which took the form of a Burns
Supper oration, written in verse and delivered in Lallans. Two
seats were contested in 1929, five in 1931, with three by-elec-
tions in between. In 1931 Nationalist candidates gained an
average of 13 per cent of the total votes cast in the constituen-
cies they contested, and in the same year they further demonstrated their claim on the loyalty of Glasgow students (for what that
was worth) by securing the election of the novelist Compton
Mackenzie as rector.

From the start two key features of official Nationalist policy
emerged: Scotland must have complete control of her own
finances, but she must also preserve friendly relations with
England. J. M. MacCormick, party secretary, was hostile to
'extremism' of any sort, whether socialistic or anti-English
(since C. M. Grieve was both, permanent feuding between the
two men ensued): it was something of a triumph for MacCormick when in 1934 he brought about the merger with the conservative Scottish Party which created the Scottish Nationalist
Party. 'It is Scotland's misfortune, not England's fault,' declared a Nationalist Party tract of 1933, 'that in the unequal

alliance she is the smaller partner.' After stressing the need for Scotland to have 'unrestricted control of her own finances' the same tract went on to discuss one of the main arguments in the anti-nationalist case, that such control would lead to the imposition of tariff barriers between England and Scotland, perhaps even to a 'military struggle':

> The spirit of Scotsmen has surely sadly degenerated since the Union, if such a fear is to prevent us from doing our best for our country and ourselves. But they need not be afraid, these doubters. The interests of even an independent Scotland would still be too closely bound up with those of her sister kingdom to permit of the slightest danger of what they seem to dread. Scotland's prosperity depends on her living harmoniously with England, and any Scottish Parliament would certainly realise that fact. For a country, to be independent is not necessarily to be bellicose.

The main base of Nationalist propaganda in the Thirties was Scotland's dismal economic condition. The slump afflicted Scotland even more seriously than it afflicted England and Wales, and it was not difficult to produce figures which suggested that Scotland was not getting a fair deal from the Imperial Exchequer. Scotland, it was argued, was, in the mid-Twenties, contributing an 'adverse balance' of at least £20 million to the British Treasury. At the same time it was apparent that in 1931–2 Scotland's total contribution to the Treasury, £67,467,500, was almost 50 per cent down on that of 11 years before, and much less than its population proportion. To Nationalists this was simply further evidence of the impoverishment of Scotland by the English; to anti-nationalists it showed how heavily Scotland, so manifestly unable to pay her way, was leaning on England. On the whole it may be said that the balance of the argument lay with the Nationalists, though as ever their problem remained that while it was possible to demonstrate that under the existing dispensation Scotland was doing badly, it was not so easy to demonstrate that with independence she would do appreciably better.

Nationalist agitation served, as Scottish Office papers make clear, to bring Scottish ills to the attention of the government. The launching of a distinct political movement, prepared to

18

contest elections, was in itself an achievement, though at no time was a sufficiently high vote polled to administer a real shock to the established political parties. Privately MacCormick entered into electoral negotiations with the Scottish Liberals, but these were aborted by the outbreak of war. The opening of St Andrew's House in Edinburgh in 1939 as the headquarters of the various Scottish departments of state was an important concession to Scottish opinion, but it was largely contrived by Sir Robert Horne, chairman of the Scottish Unionists, and, in much lesser degree, by John Buchan, novelist and Conservative politician. Some Nationalist candidates had featured such a move in their electoral addresses as a desirable immediate objective; others treated it with disdain.

On the great world issues of the Thirties the SNP shared the platform of shivering timbers thrown together by anti-Chamberlain progressives of all types. The Aberdeen branch, much influenced by Douglas Young, poet and lecturer in Greek there, gave a lead in leftist pronouncements. A sheet headed 'Scotland Needs You' read in part:

> You want a Popular Front against Chamberlain pro-Fascist Toryism . . .
> Scots voters in 1935 gave a majority for Labour, Liberal and other Progressive parties. We always do . . . Stafford Cripps supports Home Rule for Scotland. Do you?
> Why be ruled by a Tory Gang you don't elect?
> Join the Scottish Popular Front, the Scottish National Party.

Official policy was that Scotland would fight for 'liberty', 'democracy' and 'collective security' but that in the meantime she should adopt a position of 'neutrality' and oppose the introduction of conscription. The outbreak of war brought an open split, MacCormick arguing that the party must close ranks behind the war effort, Douglas Young and others founding the Neutrality League to continue advocacy of the pre-war policy. Young was sentenced to two separate terms of imprisonment for denying the right of the London government to conscript Scotsmen: his principle was 'that the Scottish people through a democratic Scottish Government should have control of whatever war effort the Scottish people wish to make.' Arthur Donaldson and one or two others were also, on various charges,

19

accorded the accolade of imprisonment by the more than usually maladroit British authorities. In June 1942 Young was elected chairman of the party by two votes over MacCormick's candidate, William Power, an elderly journalist. MacCormick's unctuous and autocratic personality is brought out by his remark (proudly quoted in his autobiography), 'I wouldn't now insult William Power by asking him to be chairman of this rabble,' and by his immediate institution of a secession movement which he called Scottish Convention.

The move was well-timed, for already a second phase in the recent history of Scottish Nationalism had begun, conveniently marked by the Parliamentary debate on the Scottish Estimates held in May 1942. Essentially this debate was a part of the widespread interest in the general problem of reconstruction aroused by the war, culminating at the end of the year in the publication of the Beveridge Report. On the basis of sentiments expressed by Scottish members of all political parties it did seem feasible to believe that all-party support could be obtained, not for the Nationalist policy of independence, but for the old Home Rule idea of federal devolution. To this policy Scottish Convention addressed itself, while the SNP continued its programme of direct political action, canalising the discontent aroused by the rigid centralised direction of the war effort and by such matters as the transfer of Scots girls to England to work in munitions factories there. In the later stages of the war it began to benefit from the electoral truce between the major parties, which meant that anti-government and protest votes, denied the formal outlet of an Opposition party, were channelled towards the minor parties. In 1943 Douglas Young came near to winning Kirkcaldy Burghs, while Dr Robert McIntyre, by winning Motherwell a year later, became the first Scottish Nationalist ever to sit in the House of Commons. Dr McIntyre, however, was swept out again in the 1945 general election, and on the whole it was Scottish Convention which made the running for the rest of the decade. A questionnaire was submitted to all Scottish candidates in the 1945 election: of 126 replies received, 79 (including two from SNP candidates) were 'favourable' to the idea of federal devolution for Scotland; three SNP candidates, along with 38 others, gave 'evasive' replies; six candidates—all Conservative or Liberal National—

gave a definite 'no'. On 22 March 1947 Scottish Convention organised its first Scottish National Assembly, attended by about 600 representatives of all political parties, trade unions and professional organisations. A resolution in favour of a Scottish parliament 'within the framework of the United Kingdom' was carried with only two dissentients (brave men!) and committees were appointed to give detailed consideration to the implications of such a resolution.

According to the Scottish Convention proposals, approved at a second National Assembly in March 1948, a Scottish parliament would be sovereign in all matters save those enumerated in a 'Schedule A', namely: the Crown and related matters; peace and war; defence services; foreign affairs and extradition; dominions, colonies and overseas possessions; treason and alienage; currency, coinage, legal tender and weights and measures; electoral law in relation to the United Kingdom parliament (the first Scottish parliament would be elected on the existing franchise, but this the same parliament might subsequently alter). Posts, telegraphs, lighthouses, docks and harbours and similar matters (enumerated in 'Schedule B') would be administered 'jointly by each parliament'. Most significant were the proposed financial arrangements, subsequently elaborated in the Scottish Convention programme, *The Financial Basis of Scottish Government* (1949). Basically the idea was that direct taxation should be in Scottish hands, but customs, excise and so on would be reserved to the United Kingdom parliament, so that there would be no question of a customs barrier between the two countries. Though the Scottish Convention case was that 'on balance the economic facts undoubtedly support the case for self-government,' no wild claims were made on behalf of the Scottish economy: thus the obvious and laudable intention of getting the best of both worlds would in effect depend on a high level of English good will. Between the two countries 'there should be no great variation in the standard of the Social Services.' Unemployment should be regarded as a joint responsibility and the burden equalised. There should be a special adjustment on account of 'the very prejudicial effects on Scottish interests of the oppressive duty on whisky'. Finally, with great realism, Scottish Convention recognised that

21

there will still be a concentration of wealth and activities in London, a continual southward drain of Scottish-derived money and its disbursement in England, to the enrichment of the latter and the encouragement of her trade.

'These facts,' it declared optimistically, 'should be taken into account in any financial arrangements made between the Scottish and United Kingdom Governments.'

The great weakness in Convention proposals was the failure to appreciate that a true federal solution implied a local parliament for England as well as Scotland. In a simple dichotomy between a Scottish parliament and a UK parliament Scotland would still be at an enormous disadvantage and, conceivably, no better off than she had been without any parliament at all. The blatantly unsatisfactory condition of Ulster was one from which Home Rulers preferred to avert their eyes.[1]

Convention's triumph was the Scottish Covenant, conceived at Aberfoyle in April 1949. In impressive if not always impeccable prose, the Covenant declared:

> We, the people of Scotland who subscribe this Engagement, declare our belief that reform in the constitution of our country is necessary to secure good government in accordance with our Scottish traditions and to promote the spiritual and economic welfare of our nation.
>
> We affirm that the desire for such reform is both deep and widespread through the whole community, transcending all political differences and sectional interests, and we undertake to continue united in purpose for its achievement.
>
> With that end in view we solemnly enter into this Covenant whereby we pledge ourselves, in all loyalty to the Crown, and within the framework of the United Kingdom, to do everything in our power to secure for Scotland a Parliament with adequate legislative authority in Scottish affairs.

Within a week the Covenant had been signed by 50,000 Scots, within two years it had almost two million signatures—striking evidence of that basic Scottish sentiment mentioned at the beginning of this essay. In 1950 representatives of the Convention

---

[1] For an admirable recent restatement of the Convention position see H. J. Paton, *Claim of Scotland* (1968).

22

(or Scottish Covenant Association, as it now called itself), re-fused the direct access to Attlee and Churchill it claimed, inter-viewed Hector McNeil, Labour Secretary of State for Scotland, and James Stuart and Walter Elliot, Conservative spokesmen on Scottish affairs. The Labour government responded with the Catto Committee, whose task was to determine whether it would be possible to publish statistics on the financial relations between England and Scotland, and the Conservatives promised a Royal Commission.

From this point on the Covenant Association was faced with the glaring problem of what to do next. It did not, as an Association, fight elections, though MacCormick had contested Inverness in 1943 as a Liberal, then, with supreme disregard for the suspicions his actions inevitably aroused, in January 1948 he secured Conservative support for a straight fight against Labour in Paisley. In September 1952 the Association put before its supporters the idea that they should give a pledge that in any succeeding election they would vote for whichever candidate most favoured Home Rule; since such a pledge came directly into conflict with ingrained party sentiment, an alternative pledge to work within existing parties for the adoption of a Home Rule programme was suggested. But supporters were rapidly ebbing away anyway: the process of befogging the issue, begun by the Labour government, was continued by the Con-servatives with their Royal Commission 'to review, with re-ference to the financial, economic, administrative and other considerations involved, the arrangements for exercising the function of His Majesty's Government in Scotland'; tartan tories returned loyally to the ministerial fold; agin-the-govern-ment elements turned again to Labour.

Meanwhile the SNP had continued to plug away, pausing from time to time to pour contempt on the Covenant movement. In the late Forties, as such tracts as Arthur Donaldson's *Exports: Opportunity or Menace?* and Tom Gibson's *Officialdom is the Curse of Scotland* demonstrate, much of its propaganda was directed against the economic policies of the third Labour government; peacetime conscription was also opposed as being 'contrary to Scottish traditions'. Actually the hollow victories of the Covenant Association played a big part in the eventual resurgence of the SNP, confirming 'straight-line' members like Dr McIntyre in their belief that Scottish ends could only be achieved directly through the ballot box, and influencing others to join up with the party. One such recruit was Mrs. Winifred Ewing, later Scottish Nationalism's second representative in the House of Commons. 'There seemed no easy way to get a Scottish government,' Mrs Ewing has said. 'I decided that the only method was that adopted by the SNP—to fight elections and win on democratic terms.'

Certain dramatic events of the early Fifties do not seem to have done much for either Covenant Association or SNP. On Christmas Day 1950 three students, whose affiliation was with the Covenanters rather than with the Nationalists, removed the Stone of Destiny from Westminster Abbey, depositing it the following April at Arbroath Abbey. On 28 November 1952 a pillar-box bearing the cypher EIIR was unveiled in the Inch housing estate in Edinburgh; after one or two unsuccessful attempts upon it, it was blown up at 10 p.m. on 12 February of the following year. Mysterious callers took to phoning the police with messages about the SRA or the Hundred Men, though the existence of either organisation was never established. Speaking on behalf of the SNP, Dr McIntyre declared:

> It is of the greatest importance that no element of terrorism enters into the Scottish Movement, but, unless the Government gives due weight to the representations of responsible people, we are powerless to prevent the actions of those who feel frustrated by the present implacable hostility of the Government towards Scottish sentiment.

At the end of the same year four students were charged in the High Court in Edinburgh with conspiring to further by criminal means 'the Scottish Republican Army or some other organisation unknown with the intention of coercing or overthrowing Her Majesty's Government'. On this charge the defendants were found not guilty, but they were sentenced to a year's imprisonment for having gelignite in their possession.

In December 1955 talks took place on the possibility of joint electoral action between the Liberals, the Scottish Covenant Association and the SNP, but nothing came of them. The *Scots Independent* became a weekly in January 1954, and at the end of 1956 the voice of Radio Free Scotland was heard for the first time over the BBC television channel. But these were the merest hints of the great revival, the third phase of modern nationalism, beginning some time in 1962. This revival is closely associated with the revulsion throughout Britain against the declining Macmillan administration. Indeed in one of its statements the SNP hit off exactly the radical technocratic image of the hour: 'the Scottish Nationalist Party stands for an independent and up-to-date Scotland, and believes this country cannot become up-to-date until it is independent.' The symbol of the 1962 revival was the West Lothian by-election in which the SNP candidate, William Wolfe, a chartered accountant, came a creditable second to Labour, and the Conservative lost his deposit. Thereafter progress was by no means consistent (the SNP in fact forfeited a deposit in the subsequent Woodside by-election), but the party felt sufficiently confident to put up 15 candidates in 1964, compared with five in 1959. There were no further significant developments until post-1966 disillusionment with Labour rule began to take effect. In the spring of 1967 the SNP poll in the Pollock (Glasgow) by-election was sufficient to ensure a Conservative victory, and in October Mrs Ewing had her great triumph at Hamilton. This victory did not necessarily mean that henceforth Nationalist candidates could count on success in similar seats throughout Scotland, but it did provide a tremendous stimulus to party recruitment (membership reached 80,000 at the beginning of 1968) and engendered a climate of confidence in which the party could contemplate making a bid in the next general election for a complete majority within Scotland.

Should the SNP win such a majority it would move immediately for an independent Scotland, either by agreement with the United Kingdom government or by secession: though party groupings might re-form later, the first Scottish government would be a Nationalist one. With Nationalists it is a matter of faith that an independent Scotland would be economically much more prosperous than she has been under Westminster rule. Differing estimates have been made of the surplus amount Scotland is alleged to contribute to the Exchequer, none of them very convincing. External trade figures are extremely hard to determine, but the probability seems to be that an independent Scotland would have an immediate balance of payments problem, which would have to be met by a lowering of living standards all round.[1] The only hard statistics at all which exist are those given in the House of Commons on 16 November 1966. These show that in almost all services government expenditure per head in Scotland is higher than in England and Wales:

| | Scotland | | | England and Wales | | |
|---|---|---|---|---|---|---|
| | £ | s. | d. | £ | s. | d. |
| Roads (including lighting) | 8 | 14 | 6 | 7 | 12 | 10 |
| Airports | | 17 | 4 | | 7 | 10 |
| Ports | | 13 | 5 | | 5 | 7 |
| Promotion of local employment | 1 | 12 | 3 | | 7 | 3 |
| Agricultural support | 5 | 6 | 10 | 4 | 6 | 10 |
| Agriculture and Fisheries services, etc. | 1 | 16 | 2 | | 10 | 1 |
| Forestry | | 11 | 2 | | 10 | 3 |
| Housing | 28 | 13 | 5 | 15 | 6 | 4 |
| Environmental Services | 13 | 16 | 9 | 10 | 15 | 3 |
| Libraries and museums | | 10 | 5 | | 19 | 6 |
| Police | 3 | 18 | 0 | 4 | 2 | 0 |
| Prisons | | 13 | 5 | | 11 | 1 |
| Other law and order (including fire services) | 1 | 14 | 2 | 2 | 0 | 3 |
| Education (other than Universities and CATs) | 27 | 11 | 6 | 24 | 19 | 8 |
| Universities and CATs | 5 | 5 | 8 | 4 | 19 | 11 |
| Health and Welfare | 26 | 18 | 5 | 24 | 14 | 6 |
| Children's services (including family allowances) | 7 | 3 | 9 | 6 | 5 | 0 |
| Benefits and Assistance | 45 | 8 | 6 | 43 | 13 | 3 |

But such arguments and figures are far from conclusive. It is perfectly conceivable that an independent Scotland, after weathering the immediate post-independence difficulties, could over a period of years build up a healthy economy on the pattern

[1] I am indebted to my colleague, Mr W. D. C. Wright, the economist, for letting me see his calculations on this matter.

of Norway or Denmark, the two countries from which Nationalists draw most solace. This seems all the more probable since
Scotland would not lumber herself with the absurd military
commitments which she has been forced to share in the past.
The existing British economy, from which Scotland would be
freeing herself, is in any event no model of fundamental good
health.

Anyway, although Nationalists believe in their economic
arguments, that is not the essential basis of their case. The en-
during theme has always been 'Scotland in Danger'; and,
despite all that had been done to meet the grievances of the
depression years, this cry was never more valid than in the
1960s, when, through emigration, Scotland was for the first
time showing a net loss of 47,000 per annum. With regard to
the question of the resuscitation of Scottish cultural and literary
traditions it is hard to be dogmatic. Back in the early Thirties
a Nationalist Party delegation, appointed to study self-government in Ireland and other countries, reported:

> One thing impressed us all. Dublin is very much *alive*. She
> has all the vigour and gaiety which one associates with a
> capital city. She is not only the seat of government and
> industry, but the centre of scholarship, letters, drama, music
> and art. Imagination pictures what Edinburgh might become
> were she to assume once more her rightful place in the
> national life as the capital of a reinvigorated Scotland.

Edinburgh is not, in the late Sixties, widely held to be 'very
much *alive*'. Is this because of a provincialism imposed by
London rule, or is it a facet of a special Scottishness which
could only be aggravated by independence? Edinburgh has its
International Festival (initiated in part from south of the border);
Edinburgh's city fathers have long failed to provide the opera
house upon which the Festival's continuing success must
ultimately depend. Perhaps it is unfair to make comparisons
between Edinburgh and London: a glance at Hull, Goole,
Derby, Sheffield or Leeds makes it clear why such a high
proportion of the English-born are happy to settle in Scotland's
capital. But by no stretch of imagination or resources could the
British Isles be made to support more than one great metropolis:
with regard to the Nationalist objectives of stimulating 'vigour

and gaiety', it might not seem an altogether good idea to sever existing connections with that metropolis. Nor indeed does the example of present-day Dublin, steadily sinking into a western sunset of priest-ridden philistinism, really give credence to the idea that political independence means cultural renaissance.

A related question to which the SNP has never given any serious attention is that of what would happen to the universities (at present incontrovertibly British institutions) in an independent Scotland; the party's one major proposal is for a new federal university with colleges in various small and rather remote Scottish towns.

These, however, are essentially matters of personal proclivity and interpretation. A much more serious obstacle to the legitimate desire to preserve Scottish manners and traditions concerns an aspect of economics, and a facet of the contemporary Irish experience, which Nationalists have preferred to ignore. It is becoming a commonplace that the hostility once felt in Eire towards the English is now reserved for the Germans, the Japanese and the Americans, providers of the capital without which, in a world of expensive technologies, all economic aspiration is in vain. Already, in communications and entertainments as well as in production and distribution, Scotland, as a small country, too often has the characteristics of 'natural' monopoly. A totally independent Scotland might all too easily become the prey of the supra-national industrial corporations.

Throughout its 40-year history the Nationalist Party has been a very heterogeneous organisation, subject to splits and given to expulsions. The easiest charge to level at it is that of fascism. In fact the party has always done its best to rid itself of the more embarrassing zealots and to place a solid perspective upon the periodic burblings about Republican Armies and gunpowder plots. A broadsheet printed for internal circulation in the late Forties and early Fifties warned party members against the dangers of strong drink and idle boasts. A similar booklet in use a decade earlier, after suggesting various slogans loyal party members might chalk on walls, had gone on to warn against indulging in 'loud controversy in tram-cars and public places'—adding, in an inspired phrase, 'especially in Edinburgh where people travel silent'. The SNP denounced Eden's Suez policies and it has been careful in its pronouncements on Rhodesia—

where traditional Scottish missionary influences serve as a counterpoise to powerful 'kith and kin' sympathies. The party can hardly be held accountable for the motives of every one of its rank-and-file members, and least of all for those of its voters: a distinction anyway must be made between the long-term membership and the youthful element captured by the glamorous image the party has recently presented. There have been occasional flashes of xenophobia. A party pamphlet of 1938 called for immigration control, the immigrants in question being Irish: 'we stand in danger of being supplanted on our own soil by the unselected and uncontrolled influx of population from Ireland.' An excessive reverence for the monarchy has been a feature of official SNP pronouncements (suggesting the lie to any possible affiliation with a Scottish Republican Army), but the sort of antiquarianism which insists that the royal family is more truly Scots than English and calls for a restoration of the Three Estaites belongs to the lunatic fringe disavowed by the party. The problem is that a party such as the SNP, given the way the odds in the existing system are stacked against it, may not in the last analysis be in a position to spurn its would-be allies and supporters, however cranky or disreputable.

In official statements of domestic policy what stands out is a sensitivity to the various vested interests mentioned at the beginning of this essay, combined with a certain mild antipathy to the organised trade union movement as at present constituted:

> The right to form and operate trade unions and trade associations will be safeguarded in the new Constitution but there must be a realisation that they are part of the nation and not its master. Intervention as organisations in politics as partisans of any party will be prohibited.

The 1934 delegation to Ireland was 'impressed by the fact that in these States business can normally be transacted in two sessions, and with Parliament sitting three days a week, thus enabling businessmen, farmers and others to carry on their own affairs.' Schoolteachers, anxious to see education freed from local authority control and returned to the *ad hoc* committees of pre-1929 days, and determined that 'reduction in the size of classes and in the number of unqualified teachers must come

29

before the raising of the school-leaving age,' have prevailed upon the party to accept both policies. Lawyers have insisted that administration in the new Scotland should be subservient to the courts. On social policies in general it would be fair to say that the SNP, in common with the major parties, has kept up with the contributions of Keynes, Beveridge, their apostles and their critics.

Developments in the authority and status of the Scottish Office, the extension in powers of the Scottish Grand Committee (1948), and the reversal since the 1940s of the utter and shameful neglect by Westminster of Scottish economic and social problems, have owed much to the pressure of Nationalists and Home Rulers alike. By the same irony through which the collapse of the Home Rule (Convention) movement in the Fifties opened the way to the striking successes of the Nationalists, so it seems likely that these very successes have now opened the way to federal Home Rule as a practicable prospect. The Nationalists have shaken the Establishment politicians and have brought a rediscovery of the old axiom that to be on the side of the angels is to be in favour of devolution. And there is nothing really incompatible between rational national sentiment and the total overhaul of the local forms of British government which is long overdue.

If we are all Home Rulers now, many of us were really Home Rulers all the time. There is, then, no need to be too cynical about the upsurge of nationalism (or, at the least, of devolutionary feeling) in strange breasts, the maturing of separate parliaments in the mind of Mr Richard Crossman, the blooming of thistles in Sir Gerald Nabarro's moustaches, the forging of claymores in the pages of the colour-supplements. It is an important point that most Scots some of the time have felt slighted by English disregard, frustrated by the remoteness of UK power, irritated by alien manners and assumptions. A recent example of such grievances is the introduction of British Standard Time, a boon no doubt in the South of England, but a mischievous nuisance in the northern part of Scotland where winter night already extends far enough into winter morning. The feeling is not absurd, and it is not new. Usually it has not, politically, amounted to much: now, partly because of adventitious circum-

30

stances, partly because of the skill and pertinacity of the Nationalist leadership, it amounts to quite a lot.

The real question for Scotsmen is not whether an independent Scotland would be viable, but whether it would be bearable.
What, that is specially Scottish, has diminished, is diminishing,
and ought to be increased? No one, Nationalist or non-National-
ist, any longer makes lavish claims for Scotland's educational
system, pre-eminent only, it seems, in the use of corporal
punishment. The Scottish universities have increasingly become
a part of the United Kingdom system administered through
the UGC; their teaching staffs contain a high proportion of
Englishmen, and have always resolutely opposed the Nationalist
desire for a university in the city of Inverness.

Early in 1968 activists at Edinburgh University forced the
resignation of their rector, Malcolm Muggeridge, whose 19th-
century upper-class accent and 19th-century religious bigotry
obviously appealed more to local citizens than to students.
Actually the Scottish universities have a rather good record
both in staff-student and town-gown relationships, but trouble
does tend to arise because respectable Scottish burghers think
of the university in their midst as, in the words of one professor
(a Scot), 'a sort of prep school' where complaints of rowdiness
or late hours can be properly reported to a headmaster. For
the livelier students (some English, some not) who tend to
monopolise student activities a Scottish city does impose a re-
strictive gloom. Still certain, most of them, that there is a life
after death, Scotland's urban middle class sees little need for
a life after dark. The Edinburgh student newspaper recently
reported in disconsolate detail upon 'half-a-night out in Edinburgh'.

Following upon the Muggeridge affair, Edinburgh councillors
indulged themselves in a wild orgy of asinine behaviour. First
they complained loudly about a private performance at the
Traverse theatre in which a half-naked girl recounted her sexual
experiences (by all informed accounts a thundering bore); they
then complained even more bitterly when, on going along ex-
pressly to view the indecent performance, they were regaled instead with an equally boring but totally unsalacious programme
which, with rare wit, the Traverse management had put on instead. It is not completely surprising if at times students seem to

set out deliberately to bait local sentiment. Then the protests flood in, pressuring the university authorities (a liberal lot on the whole) towards an authoritarian stance.

It would be unfair to associate the Scottish Nationalist Party with the Calvinist excesses of Scottish town councillors. Nationalists would argue that the narrowness of contemporary Scottish life is a facet of a provincialism created by London rule, not of a special Scottishness. Some claim that headship of the killjoy brigade properly belongs to the English puritans, not to John Knox, who was really a bit of a roisterer in his way. It must be said that in all the universities the Nationalist clubs have provided an important stimulus, not only to political nationalism outside, but to social activities within, the universities.

To many Nationalists it is an article of faith that in the last 'reform' of the liquor laws the wicked English deliberately decreed that Scottish pubs should close an hour earlier than English pubs, and should remain closed on Sundays (both changes, actually, were brought about by the joint efforts of Kirk and publicans). Possibly, as a political capital Edinburgh would also become a true cultural capital, though, as I have said, the example of Dublin does not inspire confidence in this respect. Nor does one derive great hope from the idea of a Scottish Broadcasting Corporation. Scottish broadcasting at the moment does not suffer from dominance by London, as the Nationalists claim, but from dominance by an unimaginative Scottish oligarchy producing the same programmes which constantly call upon the same pundits: Professor Esmond Wright, Dr J. Dickson Mabon, Professor John Mackintosh, Mr James Jack (of the Scottish TUC)—all gifted men, but are they the only ones? (Quite possibly they are, which is no encouraging outlook for an independent Scotland.) Scottish journalism is similarly afflicted by a closed-shop cosiness. None of this is the fault of the Nationalists. But it is hard to see how independence could fail to lead to more of the same, not less.

The first article I ever wrote for the Edinburgh student newspaper was a description of the fascist tendencies I believed existed in the Scottish Nationalist movement a dozen years ago. Hints of that are still there, in the support the movement gets from disgruntled white-collar elements, in the occasional talk of violence, in the mumbo-jumbo of secret organisations (such as the 1320 Club). But it is not the wild men of Scottish National-ism who are to be feared: it is the dull men of unchanging Scotland.

# 2

# The Three Dreams of Scottish Nationalism

## by Tom Nairn

Modern Scottish Nationalism has led a fluctuating, intermittent existence since 1853. Now, quite suddenly, it has become a more serious political reality. In the past it has gone through many renaissances, followed by even more impressive and longer-lasting collapses into inertia; but the present upsurge looks likely to last longer than others, at least, and to produce more of a mark on history.

Seen from without—from London, or in the perspective of British politics—the change appears welcome for many reasons. Like the companion nationalism of the Welsh, it brings an element of novelty into the hopelessness and corruption of the post-imperial political scene. Obviously, fringe nationalisms will be good for the English, by forcing upon them a more painful reassessment of themselves than any they have yet undergone. The smug 'deep sleep' Orwell spoke of—the fruit of the oldest and most successful of modern imperialisms—would be more disturbed by the loss of Wales or Scotland than ever it was by the loss of India or Africa. And at the moment, a particular attraction to many must seem the near-destruction of the Labour Party's power which would result from the permanent loss of their Scottish or Welsh strongholds. In the slow, festering decay of British state and society, they are the most important forces of disintegration to have appeared yet: they prefigure the dismemberment of the united British society which built up the imperial system itself. They are at once a product of the collapse of the system, and the sharpest possible comment on the advanced state of this collapse. What justice it would be, if

34

the Wilson government which came to power to 'save the pound' ended by losing Wales and Scotland as well!

Externally a positive reaction to the humiliating agony of a long era, Scottish Nationalism has another inwardness. For the Scots themselves, it is the late reflorescence of a dream, the hope of an identity, to which they have clung, obscurely and stubbornly, across centuries of provincial stagnation. Such a dream —and still more so, the time of its reflorescence—have a meaning which is bound to be far from clear outside Scotland.

Not that it seems too clearly appreciated within the country, either. Nothing demonstrates more surely the mythical nature of Scottish matter-of-factness and 'realism' than the small amount of effort the Scots have given to the prosaic understanding of what really matters to the country. Their dourness is at once a disguise, and a shield. A stony confrontation of the small change of living—counting the pence—protects them from a broader understanding that might threaten their identity: and also from what a Calvinist heritage apprehends as the sinful inner chaos. Behind the wary eyes and granite countenance of Scotland there lies not one dream only, but a whole inheritance of dreams, whose accumulation has made the psychology of modern Nationalism.

The now dominant dream of Scotland reborn should perhaps be seen as the third phase in the dream-psychology (which has very often been a dream-pathology) of Scottish history. It is deeply marked by both the great dreams that preceded it. Like them, its most important trait is a vast, impossible dissociation from the realities of history. The best short definition of Scottish history may be this: Scotland is the land where ideal has never, even for an instant, coincided with fact. Most nations have had moments of truth, at least. Scotland, never. The resultant chronic laceration of the Scots mind—most brilliantly conveyed to the world in Stevenson's fable of *Jekyll and Hyde*—is the thing which gives poignancy to the hope of a Scotland remade, when seen from within. Scottish autonomy must appear there as the healing of the secular wound which has informed—and most often poisoned—Scottish consciousness ever since the Union of 1707. The real drama of the situation lies in its potential tragedy. It is not at all evident that the forms of autonomy one can reasonably foresee—whether partial or total—could

35

cure the disease. They might perpetuate it, crystallising the long, central hopelessness of Scottish history within a framework of archaic bourgeois nationality.

But this is to anticipate. The logical place to begin is with the first tormented vision Scotland was subjected to: the Reformation. The great debate about Protestantism and capitalism established a certain affinity between the two; it has not given us any formula for the easy interpretation of the actual relationship in any given society. However, this is not too hard in, say, 17th-century Holland, or in the London or Bristol of the same period. There the immediate value and efficacy of Protestantism as the ideology of a dynamic, mercantile middle class are evident. But the case of Scotland is radically different.

The fact is that the Reformation struck Scotland long before there was any significant mercantile or capitalist development there. Two centuries later, her native bourgeoisie was not strong enough even to retain its independence. Scottish capitalism did not flourish until after the Union, in the context of the British colonial empire. Yet there is no doubt that Scotland was one of the most radically and successfully Reformed countries of Europe. The movement, which went on vigorously and progressively for over 150 years, from the time of Knox to that of the Covenanters, corresponds to the revolutions which have left their stamp on the histories and national psychologies of other countries. Four centuries have passed since the Lords of the Congregation called John Knox home from Geneva to lead this Scottish Revolution. Yet their work is still felt, in every interstice of Scottish life. Often unacknowledged now, the ghosts still preside at every feast-day there, hidden regulators of the tongue.

This religious revolution derived its power and character precisely from its historical isolation. In the dreadful, chronic anarchy and medieval poverty of Scotland, it represented the one great effort of the Scottish people towards a meaningful order of their own. The effort was separated by centuries from the material conditions which—in Weber's or Tawney's thesis—should have corresponded to it, the processes of capital accumulation. This meant that originally the Reformation movement was an absolute attempt at moral and religious order, isolated from the very conditions that would have made it an integral part of history—at once 'corrupting' it, and bestowing upon it a real historical sense. Just because it could not be the veiled ideology of a class, the Scottish Reformation was bound to be an abstract, millennial dream—in effect, a desperate effort at escape from history, rather than a logical chapter in its unfolding. The Scots wanted, and needed, Salvation in the most total sense imaginable. Scotland's Revolution gave it them neat.

The harsh absoluteness of the Scots theocracy reflected its historical displacement. It was a translation of theology into social relationships without mediation. Much more than an opiate, it provided a positive, partly democratic, intelligible social order that struck deep roots in a population whose historical experience until then had been a concentrated dose of everything worst about medieval Europe : dearth, weak central power, rapacious struggles for position, Church corruption, brigandage and wars. The divine, black dream divorced from time was also a form of civilisation As J. M. Reid notes :

> The Kirk's Elders and Ministers who supervised the behaviour of every man and woman in the parish . . . were the nearest thing to a police force that most of Scotland knew till the 19th century. It was a force not because of any physical power but because of its prestige, because the people belonged to the Kirk and believed in it, even though they might grumble or tremble when it condemned their faults.

The price the Scots payed, and still pay, for their possession by this dream was a high one. Long since, it turned into a detestable and crippling burden against which every form of creative culture has had to fight for life, from the 18th-century 'golden age' to the present day. Yet the very identity of Kirk and people— its 'national-popular' character, in Gramsci's phrase—meant that it, more than anything else, has been preserved in Scotland's long and stagnant twilight, far less than a nation yet not a province like any other. The denying demons are still alive. Addicts of the Christian-Marxist dialogue should try and shake hands with them some time, if they want to be cured.

Thus, the original character of the Reformation in Scotland was very far removed from the Weber-Tawney model. But of course this does not affect the fact that, when the conditions of capitalist development did arise in Scotland, much later, they found a country singularly well-prepared. Undoubtedly the rapidity and success of the Industrial Revolution in Scotland had something to do with this. E. J. Hobsbawm suggests in *Industry and Empire* that the Kirk's educational system was particularly important here, as well as the more general factors of ethos and psychology.

The strange, truncated condition of Scotland after 1707 made it natural to search for effective substitutes for the lost national identity. The Kirk was indeed such a substitute. But because of its unworldliness and its limitations of bigotry, inevitably an unsatisfactory one in the long run. In the later 18th century, Scotland produced two contrasting movements of culture that tried to compensate for the loss in their different ways. Basically similar to developments elsewhere in Europe, they acquired a particular meaning from the Scottish dilemma.

One was the Edinburgh Enlightenment associated with the names of David Hume and Adam Smith. This was, in effect, an escape from the peculiar destiny of Scotland, onto the plane of abstract reason (though possibly the taste for abstractions it revealed had something to do with the theological inheritance). There was a cutting edge to Hume's celebrated joke about wishing to be pardoned his Scotticisms, rather than his sins, when on his death-bed. The other movement was the same reaction to the Enlightenment as other cultures produced, towards feeling and the particular: Romanticism. It is difficult to exaggerate the importance of Romanticism for Scotland. While the Enlightenment was only an episode, Romanticism entered her soul.

Here was the second of the dreams still implanted in the sub-soil of Scottish consciousness. European history shows a general relationship between Romanticism and the nationalism of the 19th century, not entirely unlike that between the Reformation and capitalism which we have already looked at. But again, Scotland was a drastic exception to whatever generalities hold in this field. There, the new freedom of expression and the discovery of folk-culture could scarcely be the precursors or the supports of a new nation in the making (as in Italy, Hungary, Germany), nor the accompaniment of triumphant nationality (as in England and America). The Scottish nationality was dead. Scotland was once more severed from those real conditions

38

which should have lent meaning to her culture. No revolution against the humiliations of the Union, no Scottish 1848, was to furnish a historical counterpoint to Robert Burns and Sir Walter Scott. The romantic consciousness too, therefore, could only be an absolute dream to the Scots. Unable to function as ideology, as a moving spirit of history, it too was bound to become a possessing demon. Elsewhere, the revelation of the romantic past and the soul of the people informed some real future—in the Scottish limbo, they *were* the nation's reality. Romanticism provided—as the Enlightenment could not, for all its brilliance—a surrogate identity.

Perhaps this function as substitute consciousness has something to do with the peculiar intensity of Romanticism in Scotland, and with the great significance of the country as a locale of the European romantic fancy. It had the right sort of unreality. Such unreality—in effect, the substitution of nostalgia for real experience—has remained at the centre of the characteristically Scottish structure of feeling. David Craig has outlined the problem with admirable precision:

> Such nostalgia, in this 'national' form, was strong in many 19th-century literatures—in English poetry, for example, Arthurian romances and 'Merrie England' work, and in the German equivalents. It is indeed one form of Romantic escapism. What matters for integrity of feeling is the place or value this emotion is allowed to have in the whole experience, how far it is understood, and perhaps resisted.

The point is, he continues, that in Scotland it never *is* resisted, from Scott himself up to Grassic Gibbon and MacDiarmid.

> It is a mark of the uncertain foothold for a national literature in Scotland that this weak ground of nostalgia should crop up in so many places. Emigration of our most notable talents thus both creates gaps in the imaginative records of the country and tempts our writers into indulgence of their weaker sides . . . What again and again weakens them . . . is the feeling that the ground in their country is shifting under their feet, and this perhaps gets worse the greater the determination to *have* a national vantage-point, to take up one's stance inside exclusively Scottish territory.

39

A most exact historical sense can therefore be give to the assertion that Scotland is peculiarly haunted by the past. She is doubly dominated by her dead generations. At bottom there is the bedrock of Calvinism, the iron, abstract moralism of a people that distrusts this world and itself; then, overlaying this, the sentimental shadow-appropriation of this world and itself through romantic fantasy. Naturally, these strata are also in conflict with one another much of the time. But this is not the place to try and trace out the patterns of the conflict, present in some form in everything distinctively Scottish.

From this fertile soil has grown the myth-consciousness of modern Scotland, expressed in her nationalism. Nationalism is her third dream. It is basically a dream of redemption. For the Scots, national existence must represent that magic, whole reality of which they have been cheated by history—in it, their maimed past will be redeemed, in more vivid colours than a history can ever provide.

It may seem surprising that such a consciousness should have emerged from the modern history to which most historians have paid attention: essentially, the grim story of the Scottish Industrial Revolution, with the destruction of Highland society as background. Yet surely it is not. History has amply demonstrated the capacity of capitalist societies to harbour and transmit apparently archaic social forms and ideas—and, on occasion, to lend them new and monstrous life (as in Germany and Japan). For reasons not adequately studied, this sort of bourgeois society actually fosters these elements alien to itself, as counterweights to its own alienations. Surely there is no society, no landscape, more crassly impersonal and materialist than that of the Scotish industrial belt; yet this is the society which has secreted the past we have been looking at, as a dislocated and poignant inner reality.

The criterion of the success with which modern Scotland has done this is simple: the universality of its false consciousness, and the multiplicity of its forms. Scotland's myths of identity are articulated sufficiently to suit everyone. Though ministers of the Kirk, lawyers, lairds, tycoons and educationalists all have their own contrasting angles on the *Geist*, the principle articulation is between two poles. Nationalist ideology draws all its real force from one or the other. On the one hand, there is the popular—or populist—complex of ideas, which coincides enough with the foreign image of the Scots to need little elaboration here. Sporranry, alcoholism, and the ludicrous appropriation of the remains of Scotland's Celtic fringe as a national symbol, have been celebrated in a million emetic ballads. It is an image further blackened by a sickening militarism, the relic of Scotland's special role in the building up of British imperialism. Yet any judgment on this aspect of Scottish national consciousness ought to be softened by the recognition that these are the pathetic symbols of an inarticulate people unable to forge valid correlates of their different experience: the peculiar crudity of tartanry only corresponds to the peculiarly intense alienation of the Scots on this level. On the other hand, apparently (and very self-consciously!) remote from this, but part of the same machinery, there is the national consciousness of the intelligentsia. This is best seen as a sort of ethereal tartanry. Based upon rejecting the trash-image of Scotland, it aims to substitute something purer, but whose function will be the same: in effect, to seize the *real* soul of the land, beyond its blood-stained philistinism, beyond the Industrial Revolution ('This towering pulpit of the Golden Calf'), even beyond the Kirk and its progeny. The precarious sense of identity renders it intolerable to a more reflective mind that 'Scotland' should be confused with any of these things. In his 'Lament for the Great Music' Hugh MacDiarmid writes:

> My native land should be to me
> As a root to a tree. If a man's labour fills no want there
> His deeds are doomed and his music mute.
> This Scotland is not Scotland.

But then, what *is* Scotland? The fringe 'folk' culture that survived the Kirk's persecution and industrialism, and is unknown to most people now living in the country? The vivid dialect of the Lowlands, reworked into a limited poetic language by the Scots Literary Renaissance? Or some Jungian essence lying inside the living, like the dead generations, waiting on resurrection? Robert Louis Stevenson wrote, in *Weir of Hermiston*:

> For that is the mark of the Scot of all classes: that he stands
> in an attitude towards the past unthinkable to Englishmen,

and remembers and cherishes the memory of his forebears, good or bad; and there burns alive in him a sense of identity with the dead even to the twentieth generation.

There is no answer to this question. Whatever is chosen cannot possibly bear the weight put on it—be the 'root' of the tree—if one regards it prosaically, in the light of history. Perhaps this is why the Literary Renaissance had to be almost entirely poetical. Poetry in this sense is a kind of magic: it conjures up the dead and the non-existent into a semblance of the desired object. There is a profound and dangerous ambiguity in this whole movement of thought—of the greatest relevance to understanding Scotland's nationalism—which has not been sufficiently studied in the past.

First of all, it is evidently tied to the peculiarly intense romanticism we looked at above. In McLuhanite terms, one might say that the content of the new dream is the old ones, however it seems to reject the past in form. David Daiches has also pointed out how sentimentality 'lodged itself more deeply in Scotland than elsewhere, because of the division between the Scottish head and the Scottish heart that history had already produced'. Modern intellectuals are still struggling with this division. The more they get away from the stale, phoney solutions, the more obvious the sameness of their dilemma becomes. Its insolubility has the following consequences. 'This Scotland'—the real Scotland—is rejected as travesty, and can only be rejected *totally*. Here is a recent accurate gloss, by Tom Scott, on MacDiarmid's 'Lament for the Great Music':

> The Scotland of today is no longer Scotland, but a philistine travesty of itself. It is Scotshire, a county in the north of England, an ex-country, an Esau land that has sold its birthright for a mess of English pottage. . . . He, as poet, presents the Scottish people with their own image, the thing they have become, and he calls them back, like a true bard, to their own heritage. But so lost are they that they do not recognise it, or him. This is the measure of how deep the rot has gone since 1707.

What follows from such radical rejection of an impossibly corrupted reality? Either despair, as expressed by MacDiarmid:

Hauf his soul a Scot maun use
Indulgin' in illusions,
And hauf in gettin' rid o' them
And comin' to conclusions
Wi' the demoralisin' dearth
O' onything worthwhile on Earth.

Or, more sinisterly, the feeling that the 'real' Scotland which is worthwhile and has survived it all is—*oneself*. The poetical fantasy, and the poet himself, embody the sought-after *Geist*. There are then as many *Geists* as there are poets, or schools of sentimentality currently operating. Hence, a widely diffused complacent narcissism—the true mark of cultural provincialism —from which Scottish intellectuals find it hard to escape. It is a structural state of Scottish culture, with roots in the history outlined above.

This, incidentally, is what explains something that has often puzzled the external observer of things Scottish. All references —however oblique—to the more vulgar and obtrusive forms of the *weltanschauung* are met with the confident, but slightly embarrassed assertion that tartanry is now a thing of the past. It is always languishing since yesterday. This is invariably true in one sense, and totally false in another. The flexibility of Scottish narcissism simply allows transitions from the heather-clad ballad to 'Lament for the Great Music', with any number of stops in between. This is, precisely, the unity and underlying sense of a deeply defensive culture on precarious foundations that are—as Craig put it—felt as shifting under one's feet.

Inevitably, Nationalist politics are built upon this web of accreted myth-consciousness. No more striking illustration of this can be found than the common myth of Scottish Left-ness. Useful as a North Atlantic Cuba would be, the conviction that this is Scotland's destiny rests on particularly shifting ground. Scotland is certainly a more egalitarian country than England, and in some ways a more violent one. It does not follow that she is a more revolutionary one.

Scotland's gritty sense of equality derives from the old theocracy, not from Jacobinism or Bolshevism. It is double-edged, like every other aspect of that heritage. It stands for the

43

democracy of souls before the All Mighty, rather than an explosive, popular effort to *do* anything. It is extremely touchy, but passive. This passivity is intimately linked to something even more dangerous. According to the rabid forms of Protestantism that got the upper hand in Scotland, the democracy of souls is an uneasy one. Souls may be either saved or damned, and which way one goes is by far the most important question of life on earth. Regrettably, there is no rational way of resolving the problem, so that argument about it is necessarily sectarian, and endless. The only solution is by fiat, from above, by an Authority that selects the Elect from the ranks of the damned. Hence, a kind of masochism, a craving for discipline, in fact, accompanies this Scottish sense of equality. Gramsci has pointed out the analogy between Calvinist and vulgar-Marxist determinism. In fact, there is no Stalinist like a Scottish Stalinist, a truth which must have impressed itself on many students of modern British politics.

Scottish Nationalism is not in the least inherently 'Left'. It belongs squarely within a category quite familiar in the history of the world outside Scotland: bourgeois nationalism. This is, in fact, implied by the majority of Nationalist propagandists, in their favourite argument: why not Scotland? They compare the case of Scotland to those of the many new nations and nationalities which have emerged since 1945, every one of them blessed with a seat at the United Nations. Surely Scotland's 'claim' is as good as any of theirs?

Claim to *what*? This is the question that the Nationalist myth-mentality appears largely consecrated to evading, with the assistance of all hands. The right to be free, territorial self-control, even the idea of nationality itself—these are not timeless truths, but the products of a certain logic in the historical process. They occupy a broadly recognisable place in history, and have a certain justification attaching to this place. Once, the world was without nationalities—and indeed, nationality appeared, not as the expression of 'freedom' and the right to be different and unique, but as the enemy of precisely these things, the leveller of tribal and feudal variety—and it will certainly be so again. Nations and nationalisms are aspects of the bourgeois epoch of world history. Within this epoch it has (or in most cases, has had) two sorts of justification as a historical force. Firstly, as a necessary means of escape from feudal or other primitive systems that were an impossible barrier to economic and social progress. In this sense, nationalism was a precondition of the formation of modern society, and such a vital one that bourgeois civilisation has on the whole remained cast in its mould; it is only now beginning to break away from it. Secondly—mainly in the 20th century—nationalism has served as an analogous instrument for non-European societies to escape from another system which for them constituted an equally insuperable barrier to development: western imperialism. It is unnecessary here to try and discuss the complexities of these issues. But surely it is clear that in both cases nationalism had a double positive function: externally, as a means of sweeping away archaic or predatory social forms, and internally, as a means of mobilising populations for socio-economic development.

Where is Scottish Nationalism located in this perspective? In its present form, nowhere. That is, as a tragic dream comparable to the other dreams of Scotland's history precisely in its remoteness from those real conditions which could give it the historical significance it implicitly claims. Any reasonable political judgment on Scottish Nationalism must take into account both this remoteness, and its meaning in terms of Scottish history.

True to their nature, the Scots usually voice their nationalism in a very moral manner. Nowhere more so than in placing themselves within the great 20th-century anti-imperialist movement of national liberation. There can therefore be no harm in pointing out some of the moral truths which *do*, in fact, attach to the position of their country in the history of the world.

First of all, Scotland is not a colony, a semi-colony, a pseudo-colony, a near-colony, a neo-colony, or any kind of colony of the English. She is a junior but (as these things go) highly successful partner in the general business enterprise of Anglo-Scots imperialism. Now that this business is evidently on its last legs, it may be quite reasonable for the Scots to want out. But there is really no point in disguising this desire with heroic ikonry. After all, when the going was good for imperialism, the world heard very little of the Scots' longing for independence. It may not come amiss either to indicate the ludicrous phoneyness of the comparison of themselves with the Irish that the Scots are fond of in this context. The Irish rose up and wrenched their independence from imperialism when the latter was at the apex of its power. With sleekit Presbyterian moderation the Scots have restrained themselves until it is abundantly plain that the English would be incapable of stopping an insurrection on the Isle of Wight. The Irish had to fight the Black-and-Tans. The London *Times* has already half-surrendered to the Scots.

The comparison between them is not a matter of 50 years in time. It is a matter of two worlds. When, after its own grab at colonial empire had failed with the disastrous Darien Expedition of 1698, the Scottish bourgeoisie joined forces with the English in 1707, the distinction became inevitable. The Scottish people ceased to belong to Frantz Fanon's 'Wretched of the Earth'. For two centuries they have belonged to the conquerors. Their industries were, as E. J. Hobsbawm puts it, 'the cutting edge of a world industrial economy'. Their armies were the cutting edge of British imperialism. Now, the bourgeois rhetoric of nationalism blandly exorcises this history of blood and exploitation with a few readings from *The Rights of Man*. Indeed, one elder statesman of the Nationalist movement, Douglas Young, recently went on record with these remarkable words: 'The great mistake made by James VI in 1603 was to go to London. He should have governed the whole British Empire from Scotland.' Unfortunately, this vein of delirium echoes the central uncertainty of Scottish Nationalism only too accurately. When in doubt, take refuge in bombast. The Scots have become vaguely conscious of having sold their national soul to the Devil. It is more painful to recognise that the bargain of 1707 cannot now be undone, except in name—unless of course the Nationalist movement had aspirations which went beyond the terms of that bourgeois world to which 1707 and its consequences belonged. But this is another question, and one of little relevance to existing Nationalism.

Admittedly, Scotland—along with the English North-East and South-West—has also long been the victim of the unequal development characteristic of advanced capitalism. Such areas are characterised by higher, chronic rates of unemployment, poorer housing, high emigration, and generally lag behind the favoured zones of growth (like the English South-East, or the Paris conurbation). It has been recognised that one way—perhaps a necessary way—of countering this tendency is to give more power over their own affairs to these regions. The Italian Republican Constitution of 1946 remains a model for such progressive bourgeois development, although only partially enacted to this day.

But this is to confer upon Scotland's problems a status quite different from the one enshrined in the Nationalist mythology. It makes the purpose of 'independence' into a minor administrative problem. Autonomy becomes an antidote for some of the worst damage done by the reckless past evolution of the capitalist system. Looked at in this perspective, regional nationalisms could have a usefulness to the system second only to its principal support through times of crisis: the Labour Party. There is some formal analogy between such regional distortions of development within capitalism, and the world problem of 'underdevelopment'; but there is such a difference of scale and quality that it is really absurd to try and read the same political meanings into the two situations.

In a capitalist world more unified every day by the great monopolies, Scotland occupies a position of particular dependence. The regional decay resulting from her dependence upon English capitalism has only been remedied (very partially) by the invasion of American capital and its chain of light-engineering plants in the Lowlands. A bourgeois-national movement will create no new, national heaven-and-earth in this situation. It is coming into an old world whose crust hardened long ago. Its task is the anti-climactic one of administering more efficiently and humanely what was created in the past. Nationalism belongs in a young world in eruption, where the collapse of the ancient system releases visionary possibilities of a new social order forged closer to the heart. Scotland's Romantic Nationalism, which slumbered through this era of history, now emerges from its grave like a *revenant* to confront the obsidian landscape of late capitalism. Free, for the Spirit of National Redemption: the post of Local Under-Manager.

It might be objected that there are still anomalous forms of nationalism with much greater significance than this. The current nationalist stirrings of Eastern Europe, for instance, or— even more striking—France. We noticed at the beginning that Scottish and Welsh Nationalism do indeed share something of this meaning, at least in their external impact upon their context, as elements of disintegration in the aftermath of British imperialism. But they appear—so far at least—to be much less important than these other cases. In part, this is simply a matter of context. It is the sclerotic oppression of Stalinism which gives positive and liberating significance to Czech, Polish or Rumanian national movements. It is American capitalism's growing domination of Europe that lends positive historical sense to Gaullist nationalism.

In part, however, it is also a matter of the character and aspirations of the national bourgeoisie or ruling élite behind these national manifestations. After all, the French bourgeoisie, with its revolutionary traditions (however faded), its intense chauvinism and confident way of life, and its still great resources of power, is one thing. The Scottish bourgeoisie is decidedly another.

The English have curiously little grasp of this aspect of the question—as if confident that their long dominion over such provinces had necessarily produced complete mimic copies of their own ruling classes there. In Scotland at least, this naïve trust is quite unfounded. Here is one level indeed where a genuine analogy between the British provinces and the most hopeless areas of the ex-colonial Empire holds good. No West African or Asiatic *comprador* bourgeoisie has aped the external forms of English civility more sedulously—or remained more stubbornly itself, underneath them. This is the whole sense of the Calvinist mentality: cringing observance of external forms, for worldly purposes, and contemptuous disregard of them on another level. Inwardly, the Scots have absorbed little or nothing of the peculiar secrets of the English bourgeois régime: hegemony through tolerant compromise, 'permeation', the delicious mystification of traditionalism, the translation of impersonal power-relationships into subtle personal terms—all these are really closed books for them. That peculiarly heavy, gritty stylelessness, deaf to allusions and the subtler sorts of humour, that exasperating pedantry and solemn formalism, those alien and disconcerting silences and the clumsy intensity somewhere behind them tensed in relationship to a world felt as tragic and out of key with the ordinary spontaneity of living —these traits so familiar to the foreigner would be, written large, the characteristics of a Scottish bourgeois régime. They reflect that particular subordination to the past, described above. They also give a precise sense to the reactionary nature of Scottish Nationalism, and any government it produced.

The preoccupations of this parody of a ruling class are well laid out for us in A. J. C. Kerr's 1967 *Scottish Opinion Survey*. Robert Burns would be vexed (but hardly surprised) to see that republicanism is still well beyond its horizons. It is in fact deeply exercised by the difficult choice between Queen Elizabeth the I and II, and her offspring Prince Andrew, as suitable monarchs of the new realm. The real worry is the young folk, however. That odious, grudging tyranny of the older generations over youth which distinguishes Calvinism from civilisation will naturally be reinforced after independence. The truly worrying problem is: how long should National Service be in the new realm? How much of it should be military, how much enforced 'public service'? This evil *mélange* of decrepit Presbyterianism and imperialist thuggery, whose spirit may be savoured by a few mornings with the Edinburgh *Scotsman* and a few evenings watching Scottish television, appears to be solidly represented in the Scottish National Party. Those impressed by its 'radicalism' should turn to a towering portrait of the Scotch bourgeois, written in acid two generations ago by George Douglas Brown in *The House with the Green Shutters*:

> Hah! I don't understand that; it's damned nonsense!—that was his attitude to life. If 'that' had been an utterance of Shakespeare or Napoleon it would have made no difference to John Gourlay. It would have been damned nonsense just the same. And he would have told them so, if he had met them. . . . His thickness of wit was never a bar to the success of his irony. For the irony of the ignorant Scot is rarely the outcome of intellectual qualities. It depends on a falsetto voice and the use of a recognised number of catchwords. . . . Not that he was voluble of speech; he wasn't clever enough for lengthy abuse. He said little and his voice was low, but every word . . . was a stab. And often his silence was more withering than any utterance. It struck life like a black frost.

'John Gourlay' is not dead. He surfaces in all his spleen every time anything in the least 'daring' appears at the Edinburgh Festival, and keeps a watchful eye on life during the rest of the year. Nationalism may or may not have this or that radical or progressive side-effect. This rough-hewn sadism—as foreign to the English as anything in New Guinea—will surely be present in whatever junta of corporal-punishers and kirk-going cheese-parers Mrs Ewing might preside over one day in Edinburgh.

This study has not dealt with the tired legalistic arguments for independence, re-heated and served up in every Home Rule debate for the past 100 years. Anyone concerned with these fantasms—which keep Nationalist tongues wagging most of the time—will find their history in Sir Reginald Coupland's *Welsh and Scottish Nationalism*, and a good summary of them in H. J. Paton's recent *The Claim of Scotland*. Nor has it dealt with that other major obsession of the Nationalist mind: the totally Pickwickian 'economic problem' of whether Scotland would be 'viable' and could survive 'on her own'—as if she was some kind of small shopkeeper, in fact, not part of an international economic order. It has concentrated, instead, on certain aspects of Scottish history which may explain the larger depths of feeling, the structural (often half-conscious) attitudes of Nationalist psychology.

The objection that any such attempt always meets is that things are left out of it, that it fails to embrace the variety and richness of a society. In the case of Scotland, the objection is especially strong, both because of the intellectuals' revulsion against Kirk and tartan (which leads them to stress some other aspect of the country as all-important) and because of the actual variety of society there. But the point of the analysis is not to embrace and explain everything, or even to touch upon everything important. It is simply to outline the *dominant* cultural tradition: the lasting complex of attitudes derived from the historical mainstream, which asserts itself as the central reference-point, the matrix, in the system of communication that is a culture. This reference-point does not obliterate everything else, or seek to do so. Yet everything else is compelled to define its own cultural existence in relation to it, whether this relation is subordination or the utmost conscious hostility. It is the central language or idiom, whose terms everyone must begin from. It is the 'thesis' which conditions even the most extreme 'anti-thesis'—like those of the Scots intelligentsia—unless a very conscious and determined effort is made to escape from its grip.

It seems to me difficult to deny that the tradition considered here, deriving from Calvinism and Romanticism, is still a 'dominant' one in this sense, in Scotland. Indeed, it is a singularly dominant and obsessive one, quite unmistakably present in most facets of her national culture. This particularly strong hegemony is clearly related to Scotland's provincial character, to the abstraction of her culture from history in the last two centuries, and the consequent stagnation and in-growing nature of what was left. The whole problem is here. A fossilised and recessive culture is the product of Scotland's long half-life. And while this means that the country badly needs a more whole life again, so that new ferments can put an end to this stagnation, the fossilised cultural language is itself a major barrier to such wholeness. Nationalism merely ignores the problem, and this ignorance is the precise measure of its own provinciality. The belief that a bourgeois parliament and an army will cure the disease is the apex of lumpen-provinciality, the most extreme form of parochialism. As if half Europe didn't testify to the contrary!

The point of a successfully dominant tradition like the one I have tried to outline is not that it obliterates all differences and contrary tendencies—but rather, that it renders them ineffective and secondary. Of course Scotland doesn't consist entirely of John Gourlays. But the point is precisely that it doesn't have to, for his spirit and outlook to dominate things and establish the general climate of social relations and discourse. We all have a vital bit of John Gourlay inside us, and a bit of Kenneth McKellar as well, and this is enough. This means that we live in (to use Alan Jackson's brilliant, unforgettable image) the land of:

> the old Scots grim man
> with the chin
> eats an apple on the bus
>
> he hides it in his pocket between bites
> for fear of the animal
> for fear of the people.

In this land, it is also true that the spirit of the old Scots grim man has been constantly challenged, that the Kirk and our miserable tartan-waistcoated bourgeoisie have never had things *all* their own way. But the pity is, that they don't have to have things all their own way. I do not want to forget, or belittle, the popular folk tradition that has always underlain the sermons and the nostalgia. But—in the perspective of this discussion— the point is that (unfortunately) it has been forced to remain a minor, subordinate tradition of protest. I do not want to turn aside either from Scotland's native tradition of working-class protest, from John Maclean, Clydeside radicalism, or the communist tradition of the miners. But again, one is compelled to admit their lack of success, in the long battle, their failure to destroy or seriously change the character of the enemy.

It is perhaps even more important today to point out the danger to the very survival of such dissenting currents which Nationalism represents. For Nationalism appeals powerfully both to popular folk tradition and to the working class. Its essence is exactly a kind of phoney, apparently radical populism, which looks all the more radical because of its unfamiliarity in British politics. Populism unites the whole 'people' behind the image of the nation, which is everyone's birthright, everyone's property. But in fact, where it does this on the basis of a social and cultural structure like Scotland's, it really conscripts the rebels and the dissenting classes behind their old enemies. The Edinburgh baillie and the shipyard worker can both be joined in praise of Nationalism; but the nation and its culture belong to the former, not to the latter, and the triumph of a merely populist nationalism will signify a greatly strengthened grip of the real ruling class. A nationalist victory is invariably followed by an era when every form of energetic dissent or class struggle is stigmatised as treachery, the splitting of the precious and indispensable unity of the nation, the 'letting down' of the cause, and so on.

The deep, underlying strength of the nationalism of Scotland is a simple one. It is simply not possible for anyone born within the culture to resist at least part of its appeal. Nobody with any imagination can fail to be moved by the stubborn dream of true existence which has survived this desperate history without truth, this long sterility where all dreams were in vain. Misplaced, sentimental, archaic, it is nonetheless a dream of wholeness— a wholeness which will express life instead of hiding it, which will

52

free the national tongue and will from their secular inhibitions, a realness to startle itself and the watching world. It is a dream of release and affirmation, shared by many; and as such, more important than most of what passes for reality.

But what I will not admit is that the nobility in the dream bears any common measure whatever with the hideous heritage of our maimed and tragic history, and the political forces which now claim to realise the dream, without criticising this heritage. I too would like to see an end to the sad provincial stupor of Scotland. But I will not admit that this can really be achieved by a movement which wallows in the past, in the dead dreams which still haunt us, and fails even to *consider* for a moment the frightening face they have stamped upon us.

Our last dream, our dream of redemption, must necessarily be a lie, the last conclusive deception of our history, *unless it is a new dream*. We can only be 'redeemed' in fact—as opposed to the stale fantasies of what passes for our nationalism now—by a dream with a new world in it, a dream that does not re-echo the ancient ones. The true choice the Scots have is between two dreams. One which will destroy them finally, while appearing to redeem them, by shutting them within the prison of an archaic bourgeois nationality, by reinforcing their provincial and Presbyterian society, by clothing the ghosts with flesh. And the other, whose content is revolutionary, and understands that real, meaningful future existence can only be won by the destruction of these things.

We can only escape from our unreality, our historical dreamland, through a dream which places Scotland in the living mainstream of the history of our time. And this is not in the dusty mansion of SNP rhetoric—it has nothing to do with it. In the same years in which nationalism again became a force in Scotland, the western world was shaken by the first tremors of a new social revolution, from San Francisco to Prague. I for one am enough of a nationalist, and have enough faith in the students and young workers of Glasgow and Edinburgh, to believe that these forces are also present in them. I will not admit that the great dreams of May 1968 are foreign to us, that the great words on the Sorbonne walls would not be at home on the walls of Aberdeen or St Andrews, or that Linwood and Dundee could not be Flins and Nantes. Nor will I admit that, faced with a choice between the spirit of the *Mouvement du 22 mars* and Mrs Ewing, we owe it to 'Scotland' to choose the latter. On the contrary, in a country poisoned by stale authoritarianism, the universal revolt of youth against authoritarianism should have a quite special sense and value.

It is to the extent—and only to the extent—that Scottish Nationalism links itself to such new forces and ideas that it will avoid being the 'proper', suitable summing-up of the old problems. That is, the perpetuation of what we *are*, the tragic dénouement of our tragic half-history. It goes without saying that such a revolutionary nationalism can only exist by combatting the past which conventional nationalism drools over, that what Gramsci called 'pessimism of the intelligence' is its life-blood. It can only exist as a cultural liberation from Scotland's myths. To acquiesce in the SNP's version of our future, in the year where a new generation cried '*Nous sommes tous des Juifs Allemands*' before the Palais Bourbon and ground the nationalism of the past to dust at the Saarbrucken bridge, is merely an uninteresting form of suicide. I will not admit that this is the best we can do, that a party incapable of even a symbolic firecracker in the path of the annual Royal Progress to Scotland has the right to speak for *me*, as a nationalist.

Of course, one might object that the dichotomy is too sharply drawn. In any case, a nationalist triumph—even SNP-style—must bring a certain amount of social upheaval and change, and the liberation of new ideas and forces. But this doesn't lessen the choice one bit. For obviously the time to start fighting for the new ideas, with the new forces, is now, not then.

I see that Scottish Nationalism now has the benediction of our annual General Assembly of crows. It must already be dreaming of the Inaugural Procession of the new régime to St Giles, where the All Mighty will smile on it too. As far as I'm concerned, Scotland will be reborn the day the last minister is strangled with the last copy of the *Sunday Post*. I hope I'm not alone.

# 3

## *Satori* in Scotland

### by Hugh MacDiarmid

Most of my early lyrics were published in a little book on the
title-page of which I had the foresight to put: *Habent sua fata
libelli*. That anticipation has proved more than justified over
the 40 years since the lyrics were first published. In a few
quarters they were recognised immediately to be of exceptional
quality: these included the *Times Literary Supplement*, the
*Glasgow Herald* and the *Manchester Guardian*. But they were
rare in their appreciation. In Scotland itself I was subjected
almost everywhere to ridicule and abuse. Just as the Edinburgh
*literati* of the time advised Burns that if he continued to write
in Scots, he would confine his readership to a fraction of the
Scottish reading public, whereas if he wrote in English he would
be available to one that was world-wide, so I was counselled
that writing in Scots was foredoomed to failure. Not only that,
but I was not even writing in the relatively simple Scots Burns
wrote in, but in a far denser linguistic medium. This medium
(so it was thought) had been made by taking elements from the
different dialects into which Scots had disintegrated, together
with obsolete words from the 15th and 16th-century Makars,
which were no longer understood except by a few scholars.
Despite the Edinburgh *literati*, however, Burns achieved a fame
unique in literary history. And for my own part, condemned at
home and regarded in England as of no account, I was speedily
recognised abroad.

Now I may be as over-praised as I was then under-rated.
Professor David Daiches, for example, can write: 'Dunbar,
Burns and MacDiarmid are the great Scottish trio. Let pedants
wrangle over which of these deserves the precedence; there can
be little doubt that MacDiarmid is the greatest miracle.'

Similar statements have been made in various countries during the last few years, and it was a distinguished Frenchman, Professor Denis Saurat, who early on set the ball rolling: *'Il faut que MacDiarmid prenne la place de Burns. Je ne veux pas dire qui'il est un nouveau Burns. Ce serait une calamité.'* Scottish readers, however, did not want anything new, and above all they did not want Burns supplanted. It had long been generally agreed that the independent Scottish tradition was finished: it had culminated in Burns, who was the be-all and end-all of Scottish poetry. And I was warned of the dire fate in store for me if I tried to oust Burns from that position, or tried to write poems that were not imitative of his. A Moderator of the Church of Scotland denounced my work as not poetry at all, as containing much that could never have emanated from the sane and was reminiscent of nothing so much as Homer without his false teeth. In a recent essay the poet Sydney Goodsir Smith deals with what he calls 'the anti-Scottish lobby in Scottish letters'. He traces the opposition to complete cultural absorption into the British (i.e. English) totality which was shown by Burns and myself and a few others—with, as one commentator put it, 'a mad Japanese courage'—from 1771 to the present day. One of the defeatists was Edwin Muir in *Scott and Scotland* (1936), though he had spoken previously of my lyrics in terms of the highest praise. Of 'Country Life', he had written: 'It is an almost fantastic economy, a crazy economy, which has the effect of humour and yet conveys a kind of horror, which makes this poem so original and so truly Scottish.'

*Habent sua fata libelli.* What a complete somersault of opinion these short lyrics of 8 or 12 lines have effected. And the revaluation isn't over yet. Sir Compton Mackenzie thought they could bring about the regeneration of Scotland and lead to the regaining of our sovereign independence. Mr Anthony Burgess has said of me: 'Through him that nation becomes articulate again, and great rhetoric serves an end that many Sassenachs hope will be attained. I mean the liberation of Scotland, not necessarily under a Jacobite Royal, but quite possibly under a Jacobin President, who is the greatest poet at present living in these islands.'

What gave this little collection of lyrics this incredible power? How did I come to write them? I can shed little light on the matter. They just happened. If I am asked when I think I got my first idea about Scotland, I can only reply that I don't think I was ever unaware of it. As a Border man, living on the frontier, I was always acutely conscious of the difference between the Scots and the English and I had from the start a certain anti-English feeling. But the first time I applied myself to understand the position and acquire a definite idea of Scotland was after I was demobbed in 1920. That was natural enough. After all, we were fighting a war that was ostensibly for the rights of small nations, poor little Belgium and so on, and when I came back I discovered to my horror that I didn't know anything about Scotland and had never been taught anything about Scots literature. At school we were punished if we lapsed into Scots. 'Standard English' was the rule: a linguistic fiction which doesn't exist in England itself, where there are more dialects than in Scotland—dialects, morever, which are determined by social status, a state of affairs not found in any other country. Yet most of the people in my home town spoke Scots—my own parents certainly did. So Scots was really my native language. Apart from one or two of the more hackneyed love songs of Burns and the like, however, we got nothing at all at school about Scottish literature and very little about Scottish history.

I am generally credited with having been instrumental in changing all that. A few years ago the Scottish Education Department decreed that dialect (as they called Scots) was to be encouraged in the classrooms. This policy it was found impossible to implement, save in isolated cases, because the majority of the teachers themselves were hopelessly over-Anglicised and didn't know it. Nor could they teach Scottish literature because they themselves had never been taught how to judge it. More recently, however, courses in Scottish literature have been established in most of our universities as part of both the ordinary MA and Honours curricula, and an increasing number of students are now graduating in the subject: my *Drunk Man* has been used as a textbook in these classes. Glasgow Education Authority decreed not long ago that Scottish literature must now be taught in all the city's primary and secondary schools. This is surely a remarkable reversal of policy after two and a half centuries during which English literature and language were given a virtual monopoly. And this reversal can be seen as a sign of the times, now that the remarkable upsurge in membership of the Scottish National Party has made it the largest political party in Scotland and a serious challenge to the three older ones.

I have called this article '*Satori* in Scotland' because *satori* is 'an illumination, a sudden awakening'. Mine was quite unheralded. I had never had any intention of writing poetry in Scots, though I had never had much liking for any English poetry and even in my final years as a schoolboy was quoting Rimbaud, Verlaine, Verhaeren, Richard Dehmel, Else Lasker-Schüler and Renée Vivien in my essays. I have never had much to do with English writers either, but I received great encouragement in the early days, when I needed it most, from Irish writers like Yeats, A. E., Gogarty, Shaw and, above all, Sean O'Casey. Of all the writers I have known personally, O'Casey was in many ways the closest to me.

The Vernacular Circle of the London Burns Club was agitating for the preservation of Scots, but I knew they conceived it only as a medium for the continuance of post-Burnsian doggerel, banality, jocosity and mawkish sentimentality. All of which I hated like hell. I could think of no other literature which had plunged into such an abyss of witless rubbish as had Scots poetry after the great achievements in the 15th and 16th centuries of poets like Dunbar, Henryson and Gavin Douglas. The Burns cult appeared to be largely to blame, so I opposed the Burns Club's proposals. And then I suddenly wondered if I was being quite fair. It might all depend on the angle from which one approached the question of exploring the expressive potentialities of Scots as a medium for the whole range of modern literary purpose. The language had disintegrated into dialects, but perhaps these could be more or less arbitrarily combined and so provide a basis from which it might be possible to work towards reconstituting a full canon for the language.

So I went to where the words were—to Jamieson's *Dictionary*. My early poems were written straight from that source. They came to me very rapidly, and were generally completed in my head while I was going about my day's work as a journalist, and then written down when I got home at night. As Leon Vivante says, in poetry 'the words find by themselves a thousand avenues, the deepest and truest conceptual affinities; they re-connect forgotten kinships.' This is precisely what happened in my case.

The creation of these lyrics—the whole business of my turn-ing to Scots—was an accident, if you like; it was certainly a phenomenon akin to religious conversion. I just suddenly felt as a Scot what J. S. Machar confesses in his 'Tractate of Patriotism': 'My Czechdom is the portion of my life which I feel, not as delight and bliss, but as a solemn and inborn fealty. My native land is within me alone . . .' And the experience I underwent is exactly described by Ford Madox Hueffer:

> What is the love of one's land? . . .
> It is something that sleeps
> For a year—for a day—
> For a month—something that keeps
> Very hidden and quiet and still
> And then takes
> The quiet heart like a wave
> The quiet brain like a spell
> The quiet will
> Like a tornado: and that shakes
> The whole of the soul.

My so-called disciples have seldom got beyond mere diction-ary-dredging to achieve the illumination which I have called *satori*. Almost all our contemporary poets in Scotland have developed two rather intractable defects or diseases, and every-thing as far as the future of Scots poetry is concerned depends on these being cured. The first is a sort of osmotic reluctance, on the part of their mental perceptions, to step through the cilia of what *seems* to be, and reach the vital stream of what actually is. The second is the lack of correspondence, or the essential incongruity, between the words they try to use and the way their minds work, so that their verse is afflicted by a species of *aniseikonia*: a word derived from Greek words meaning 'un-equal imagery' and usually applied to the distressing conse-quences which sometimes result from the fact that images carried to the brain by the two eyes can be quite different both in size and shape. This defect, amongst other things, prevents some people, even of fair intelligence, from comprehending what they read.

Even those writers who have a good knowledge of Lallans are divided between it and the English to which they are so hopelessly over-conditioned. As with the difference between the right-eye and the left-eye images, such writers—and readers—in passing from Scots to English, and from English to Scots, have a violent struggle to equate the two things. It must be admitted that all of these readers and writers can only be described as hard-of-thinking—which is the main problem confronting our movement.

Scots—or Lallans, as Burns called it—has a positive advantage simply through being so long disused, or unfamiliar in print: the eye does not run over it so easily but is arrested every now and again and compelled to debate the significance of this or that word. While men like Professor H. J. C. Grierson and John Buchan found it astonishing that 'the speech of simple peasants' could be used successfully as a medium for metaphysical speculation, this was simply because Scots had been so long neglected for the purposes of high poetry, and because they thought of it as just a rustic dialect, instead of a language in the fullest sense of the term (*in posse* if not *in esse*), as I did. The late Sir Alexander Gray was an exemplar of a point of view diametrically opposed to my own in this matter. He was particular about dialect demarcations and believed that if Scots was to be used as a literary medium, this must be done with the authentic usage, limited vocabulary and typical ideas (or lack of ideas) of the sort of people who actually spoke it. Edwin Muir denounced the attempt to write in Scots, declaring that the people who did so thought in English, and that there was thus a fatal division between their mentality and their mode of expression. An even worse disease than *aniseikonia*, no doubt. He instanced the passage in *Tam o' Shanter* which begins, 'But pleasures are like poppies spread . . .' as representing the case of a Scottish poet, with thoughts that were incapable of expression in Scots, finding it necessary to deviate into English. Muir failed to realise that my own tendency was in precisely the opposite direction—to deepen into quite untranslatable Scots rather than, like Burns, to modulate into English.

# 4

# The Heart of the Cabbage

## by Louis Simpson

One June I flew to Scotland to see Hugh MacDiarmid. I had
been reading the *Collected Poems* and everything else by Mac-
Diarmid I could find in the New York libraries. But I could
find no critical study of his works. Then I had the idea of writing
one myself. I wrote a letter to Robin Lorimer in Edinburgh,
who had edited my study of James Hogg, asking his advice.
Lorimer answered that a great deal had been written about
MacDiarmid, but most of it was superficial, and he proposed
that I come to Edinburgh and 'get to know Chris, who is always
very receptive to people who are genuinely interested in him
and his work'.

There is a society in New York that gives money to poor
scholars. I went to their offices and told the director that I must
go to Scotland at once. MacDiarmid was a great poet, neglected
in America, and I wanted to gather materials for a book. The
director said that it was late to apply. Wouldn't next year do?
No, I said, I must set off at once. The director told me to put
my application in writing and also to get a letter from Mac-
Diarmid saying that he would see me. In answer to the letter I
wrote, MacDiarmid said that he would be 'available—and delighted'.

So, at a height of 37,000 feet and a cruising speed of 520 to
580 m.p.h., I approached MacDiarmid's Scotland. The night
was dark with a few diamond-hard stars. This paled to blue-
green and a red line with a long streak of cloud.

> Mars is braw in crammasy,
> Venus in a green silk goun,
> The auld mune shak's her gowden feathers . . .

Two hours later I woke in bright sunlight, above a surface of ridged, grey clouds. Then there were breaks, abysses, where the blue sea was. I turned to MacDiarmid's later poems in English. They seemed appropriate to this flying:

> Sound shrinks to nothingness and musical composition
> Becomes an abstract philosophical activity.

When I got to Edinburgh Robin Lorimer was absent in London, so I spent a few days wandering about, renewing my acquaintance with the town. The King's Theatre was playing 'Five-Past Eight '63, the Fast-Moving, Song, Dance and Laughter Show'. I bought a ticket and watched a spectacle MacDiarmid would have detested. It was all a parody of movies: dancers in 'Western' costume against a background of hanging wagon-wheels and fence rails. A woman bawled a song, 'I've got your number', the words and gestures heavily Americanised. Then, God help us, there were songs 'that had been awarded American Oscars', with appropriate scenery and chorus routines. I escaped during the intermission. On the way back to my lodging-house as I passed the gardens between the Castle and Princes Street there was a lighted platform on which kilted dancers were dancing to the pipes. I was no judge of piping and dancing, but I could see the difference between this and what was going on at the King's Theatre. This was pleasure; the other a Paradise of Fools, whirling to the gusts blown out of Tin Pan Alley.

> We have no use for the great music.
> All we need is a few good-going tunes.

One evening I met Sydney Goodsir Smith in the Paper Bookshop off George Square. We talked about poetry and he said: 'American poets are lucky. You can get published.' We talked about prose, and he said that the American tradition was the 'fiction of space', as in Mark Twain, Whitman and Wolfe. I told Smith that I didn't find American 'expansiveness' in his own poems, but wildness, as in his 'Meth-Drinker' poem, a wildness strictly controlled. Smith said he was a classicist: he wanted 'the concentration of feeling that explodes and goes straight upward'. I said he seemed more lyrical than MacDiarmid was nowadays. 'Don't compare me with MacDiarmid,' he said. 'I look at a man's shoes—MacDiarmid, at a man's dreams in the air.' By this time we had moved on to a bar where Smith bought whisky for both of us and also three strangers. These people, good middle-class Scots, looked at Smith with a mixture of curiosity and some other feeling I could not place.

The next day Robin Lorimer was back from London. We went together to Milne's pub in Hanover Street, and there we met MacDiarmid. He was on his way to a wedding reception. I had an impression of white hair, a wide brow, clear eyes, a white complexion. He talked Scots-English and he was in a twinkling mood. Robin and I had come into the middle of a conversation about Christine Keeler and the current Tory scandal. 'Sexual promiscuity,' said MacDiarmid, 'I'm all for it, but I've never encountered it myself.' A little later he told me, looking around the pub: 'I've been a caterpillar crawling on the edge, but this is the heart of the cabbage.' I told MacDiarmid that when I was in New York I had met a man who knew him. He had a collection of MacDiarmid's works, and offered to let me look at them and also to give me an introduction. But on my next meeting with the man he had become very secretive. Oh yes, MacDiarmid said, he had known the man in the Thirties; he had gone to Spain. As for his unwillingness to help me, 'people have a sort of proprietary interest in me, you know.' Robin asked if it would be all right if we brought out a tape-recorder when we had our interview, and MacDiarmid said yes. 'I'm all for publicity—but Christine Keeler, I wouldn't like that sort of thing.'

On 2 July in the morning Robin and I drove to MacDiarmid's cottage at Candymill. The 'haar' was over the country and the road, and there was a light drizzle. Chris answered the door. He said that his wife Valda was absent, having made a previous appointment. He let us into the small living-room and offered me a chair near the fire, from which he ejected his dog. Its name, he said, was Janey. A neighbouring farmer had a dog of the same species, and Chris had thought he'd be getting 'a pound a pup', but this dog turned out to be 'a pure hermaphrodite'. It was a friendly creature, though frustrated.

We settled down facing each other. Robin put the tape-recorder on a table to my left and the microphone on another table to Chris's right. We began to talk. I started with a sentence from MacDiarmid's autobiography, *Lucky Poet*, and asked him

to explain it: 'The true poet never merely articulates a precon-
ception of his tribe, but starts rather from an inner fact of his
individual consciousness.' Chris talked of his boyhood in Langholm, his beginnings as a poet, his parents, his attitude to religion, his service in World War I, the Scottish Renaissance,
and other matters. I asked him to read from his early poems in
'Synthetic Scots'. He put on his glasses and read with enjoyment
and feeling. I said I was afraid of wearing him out. 'No chance
of that,' he answered, and laughed. Then we talked about his
years as a journalist, his communism, his life in the Shetlands,
his experiences as a shipyard worker in World War II, his paci-
fism, and his Anglophobia. I asked him to read also from his
poems in English, and he did, with a long extract from 'Direadh
III'. He stopped reading because his mouth was 'filling with
spit'. He had his false teeth out and he said that without his
teeth he could not cut off his words as clearly as he'd wish to.

He was solicitous; he offered to make tea and was sorry Valda
was absent. He said that there were six visitors the day before,
and if he had a telephone he would be answering all the time.
He had a slight and winning vanity—rather, it was as though he
were not quite sure that I knew how important he was. When I
showed him a review of his *Collected Poems* in an American
magazine he told me there had been 40 or 50 reviews that he
had copies of, but there were few intelligent reviewers.

As he talked I tried to memorise his features. His face, as in
the good photographs, was wide with a great brow and prominent jaw, the whole face receding from the jaw. The eyes were
gentle among their wrinkles. When I asked him a question he
attended carefully, looking into my eyes. He cupped a hand
to his left ear to hear better. Sometimes he turned to Robin
for him to explain what I meant. He would answer to the point,
then digress. He talked about the people who, hearing that his
cottage was in need of repair, had come out to Candymill with
tools and materials and worked on the cottage and made it
habitable. For a man who had once written 'I have had to get
rid of all my friends,' Chris seemed better provided with friends
than anyone I had ever met.

During our conversation he rose to get a book, one of his
own, entitled *The Islands of Scotland*. He couldn't find it. 'If *I*
put the books somewhere, I can find them,' he said. But Valda,

1. *Hector MacIver*

2. *Norman MacCaig, 1965*

3. The Royal High School, seen from the Canongate Churchyard in 1829. From a print by Thomas Shepherd; engraved by J. Henshall. Regent Road passes in front of the School

it seemed, had put it somewhere. Was it in one of the boxes under the couch? We pulled out two boxes, bumping our heads together, but couldn't find the book.

Late in the afternoon I asked him if he would like to come to the States. I had talked of this with Elizabeth Kray of the Academy of American Poets, and she was interested. Chris said he would very much like to come to America, but—and he looked serious—Mrs Grieve would not like his coming. She would be afraid of the same thing happening to him that happened to Dylan Thomas. 'I was a close friend of Thomas.' I told him that an effort would be made to bring Mrs Grieve over too. 'Then it would be all right,' he said, 'but would I be able to get in?'—meaning his communism and the attitude of the American State Department. I said that if Mrs Grieve and he were willing, and if Betty Kray could arrange for a reading, then an effort would be made to clear the matter with the US government. He asked me to come back whenever I felt like it. He was quite free for a few weeks.

Robin and I had some trouble getting the car started on the grassy verge of the road, about 50 feet from the house. Chris walked out and got behind the car to push. He was 71 years old, the ground was muddy, and I had a feeling that a disaster might occur. I did not want to be the American who had come all the way to Scotland to disable a poet. I asked him to stand aside. Finally the car got going and Chris waved us off.

Robin and Priscilla Lorimer had invited me to move from my lodgings to their house in Sciennes Gardens. There I wrote home my first impressions of Christopher Grieve: 'I had the impression of being in the presence of a truly great man and poet—the first, in my experience, to combine both qualities.'

In the days that followed I tried to buy MacDiarmid's works. But it was impossible to find copies of the early books. I left my name with the booksellers and a message for Kulgin Duval who, I had been told, was collecting MacDiarmid material. Then Robin arranged for me to have an interview with the poet Helen B. Cruickshank, who had been for many years a friend of MacDiarmid. She invited me to spend a day with her looking through her correspondence. On the fifth of July I went out to her house and was received warmly by a handsome woman in her seventies. We talked about my plan to write a book. As

E 65

we were talking I saw on a shelf behind her a line of first editions of MacDiarmid. I began shaking with buck fever, the nervousness felt by hunters who sight a deer and are afraid that some precipitate movement on their part will cause it to dash off. I asked Helen Cruickshank if she would sell me any of the books, for I needed them desperately for my work. She said yes and lifted down the volumes I named. She looked at the price marked on a book-jacket and asked if I were willing to pay that much. I pointed out that the book in her hand, *Lucky Poet*, for which she was asking $3.50, was worth at least $25, and I could not pay less. She said that she was not interested in making money, that when she died her possessions would be dispersed and, besides, she liked me. Then we sat in the garden and had tea and the birds came. The garden was full of flowers, foxgloves and roses: there was a birch tree like the birches outside my cabin in California.

She brought out a box containing 75 letters from MacDiarmid or relating to MacDiarmid that she had collected over the years from 1922 to 1962. I asked if I might make copies. She said yes, and I set about it, writing as fast as I could. I was trying to get everything down—the facts about his early struggles as a writer and his poverty when he lived on the island of Whalsay in the Shetlands: 'The core of the problem . . . is the difficulty in maintaining our credit accounts here for such daily essentials as milk, bread, and paraffin oil, until such time as I can get my books—or some of them—finished and sent in to the publishers.'

Then I began getting writer's cramp. I asked Helen Cruickshank, again with apprehension that it might be refused, if I might take away all the letters and have photostats made of them. She had said that just a few days ago a man had visited her and gone through the letters and taken away the ones he wanted. I told her that the collection was valuable and copies should be made immediately and placed in the National Library before other visitors helped themselves. She said I might borrow the collection for this purpose.

I took the letters away, and had two sets of photostats made. I asked Robin Lorimer to place one set in the National Library. I kept the other set myself, and returned the originals to Helen Cruickshank.

At my second interview with Chris, Valda was present. She

was, as we say, loaded for bear. She told me that she did not approve of people who came to see Chris, interviewed him and made him record his poems, and made promises which they did not keep. I told her that my intentions were honest and that my main reason for seeing Chris was that I admired his poetry. Then she tore into Americans. Referring to the crisis during which the United States had brought pressure on the Soviet Union to withdraw their rockets from Cuba, she said that in her opinion the rockets should have been launched against the United States. I said that such a course of action would have entailed the destruction not only of the United States which she detested, but also of the USSR which she admired. Then she got onto the subject of the treatment of Negroes in the United States. The only Americans she had ever met whom she liked were American Negro soldiers stationed in Scotland during World War II. They had exquisite taste. At this point I shook my head. 'Are you anti-nig?' she said. I had never heard the expression, but in a moment I understood it, and told her that I was objecting only to her description of Negroes as a type.

I knew something about Valda's life with Chris, particularly their years of isolation in the Shetlands, and I could understand her resentment of a visitor coming from America. Communism had not been just a theory to the Grieves. They had lived it. For many years it had been difficult for Chris to find a market for his poems, articles and books. His opinions offended many people. His pleading for Scotland offended 'the English Ascendancy, the hideous khaki Empire'. His dogmatic Marxism offended others. Naturally both Chris and Valda were anti-American. In the Marxist fable the US is a capitalist state inhabited by only two kinds of people, the oppressors and the oppressed. But I was not here to explain the United States, and in any case people who have a fixed system of belief do not wish to hear anything to the contrary.

Valda gave us lunch, and then we stopped trying to make a business-like recording of poems and a series of questions and answers. The conversation degenerated, or perhaps it rose, to the level of gossip. Weeks later, back in America, when I had the interviews transcribed by a stenographer and looked them over, I realised they were almost entirely worthless. I had not got from Chris anything that he had not already expressed more vividly in his books. I wished that instead of trying to be a reporter I had just spent my time talking to him about poetry. Nevertheless, I submitted the manuscript to the *Paris Review*, at the editors' invitation. They did not publish it. Then I asked them to return the manuscript, but I never received it.

There was a great book waiting to be written about Christopher Grieve—a study of his life and works. It would have to be, also, a study of Scottish culture over half a century, for Grieve had been involved in several movements of that culture. But I realised that I did not have the knowledge to undertake the task, nor was I temperamentally suited. To write such a book what was needed was a *Scottish* Boswell.

Then why not forget the man and just write about the poetry? The trouble was MacDiarmid's didacticism. Once he had written:

> Better a'e gowden lyric
> Than a social problem solved.

But in later years he turned sharply against this attitude. He spoke with contempt of readers who wished that he would write lyrics as he used to; they were 'seductive voices' that he must not heed. As time passed he became more devoted to communism, and the dialectic could not be separated from his poetry. As he told me, 'if the communist dialectic gets thoroughly into you, into your blood and bones, as it is in mine . . .' Long stretches of his poems were political tracts. I would have thought them tedious no matter what kind of opinion they were propagating, but communism was a belief I found singularly unattractive. Whatever communism might be in theory, I could not sympathise with MacDiarmid's praise of its manifestation in the Soviet Union. Under that system of government men who spoke out were silenced. And when MacDiarmid approved of this—

> What maitter't wha we kill
> To lessen that foulest murder that deprives
> Maist men of real lives?

—my sympathy failed. I could not stomach opinions such as these, and in MacDiarmid's poems they were not translated into narrative or song—they were preached straight at the reader.

I thought MacDiarmid had mistaken the source of his

strength. Instead of echoing communist dogma he should have stuck to Scotland, the heart of the cabbage. It was Scotland that made him and would understand him at the last. His best writing was about the places where he lived and the friends and enemies he had. It was Scottish ways of thinking that gave his poems their vigour. What on earth did the working-class poet from Langholm have in common with the politicians in the Kremlin? MacDiarmid had undertaken to support a totalitarian system of government that was a means of enslaving men. But the Scotland in his poems was true and would endure for ever—at least while men loved freedom and had the heart for a song. MacDiarmid's strength was in the fusion of his personality with the pride and despair of Scotland. When this fusion occurred, his poetry was powerful, wild, ranging in thought; he combined lyrical and argumentative powers. At the end of 'Lament for the Great Music' he had the force, and by his devotion to Scotland he had earned the right, to summon the great pipers:

standing shoulder to shoulder
With Patrick Mor MacCrimmon and Duncan Ban
    MacCrimmon in the centre
In the hollow at Boreraig or in front of Dunvegan Castle
Or on the lip of the broken graves in Kilmuir Kirkyard
While, the living stricken ghastly in the eternal light
And the rest of the dead all risen blue-faced from their
    graves
(Though, the pipes to your hand, you will be once more
Perfectly at ease, and as you were in your prime)
All ever born crowd the islands and the West Coast of
    Scotland
Which has standing room for them all, and the air
    curdled with angels . . .

# 5

# The Scottish 'Renaissance' of the 1930s

## by George Scott-Moncrieff

It was Hugh MacDiarmid who first used the expression 'Scottish Renaissance'. This was in the middle 1920s, when MacDiarmid was associated with Neil Gunn and Edwin Muir in producing the *Scottish Chapbook*. Perhaps it was rash, premature: one should be canny speaking of a birth until it has actually happened. Yet so long as there is life, always, everywhere, things struggle, like Yeats's rough beast, to be born, or reborn.

It was inevitable that the Union of 1707, humiliatingly entered into by the partner in the north, should continually rankle there in some measure. Both Fifteen and Forty-five were owed in part to resentment against an incorporating union that made Scotland subservient to England. Then there was a rankling at some of the forms the original rankle took, the 'whae's like us?' cry of chauvinistic self-assertion, that stimulated the idea, the hope, of a renaissance.

Home Rule associations of various kinds were numerous over the years. They produced many short-lived publications, forgotten except when occasionally dug out of the archives by busy beavers writing theses for American or German universities. Compton Mackenzie in his *Sixth Octave* gives chapter and verse for the founding of the Scottish National Party in 1928. It was effectively the work of John MacCormick, the law student at Glasgow University who was 'able to convince various seniors like Lewis Spence and R. E. Muirhead that if the National movement was to make real headway it was vital to amalgamate the various Home Rule associations already in existence into what should be called the National Party of Scotland'.

70

Lewis Spence was himself a poet, and other writers were quickly associated with the new, unifying movement. Cunninghame Graham, that splendid romantic figure, was politician as well as writer. As an MP, pioneer of the Labour Movement, he had gone to prison along with John Burns some 40 years earlier when the police beat up a rally in Trafalgar Square in 1887. His was the tradition of the aristocratic revolutionary— freed, by the assurance of the status of his birth, to take an independent line. His socialism was, like that of his colleague, Keir Hardie, a radical call for social justice rather than the doctrinaire, Marx-infected socialism that succeeded it; equally it demanded Home Rule for Scotland and Ireland.

Cunninghame Graham was a short-story writer and essayist, (he has a superb description of the House of Commons squirming beneath the Irish irony of Parnell): Compton Mackenzie as a novelist had a much wider popularity. Then aged 45, he had newly come to know Scotland and found that the country of his forebears had a fresh savour, that uniqueness belonging to each of its constituent parts that has been the source of Europe's greatness and inexhaustible interest: not a matter of being better than other parts but of being different and therefore able to offer other insights into the human conspectus. The ardent upholders, left or right, of a vanished imperialism seem not to notice, even today, that far from being a retrogressive step, 'putting the clock back', a desire for smaller units of responsibility is the dominant trend in an age that has tasted the fruits of the political empires of Hitler, Stalin and Mussolini, and the commercial empire of the USA.

Yet for all the veteran revolt of Cunninghame Graham and the spirited good sense of Compton Mackenzie, the figure who dominates the Scottish Renaissance, if we admit the term even although the event never did manifest itself as the young of that and many later days hoped, must remain that of C. M. Grieve, Hugh MacDiarmid.

Poetry, when it is good enough, has a trigger-like quality, even although the explosion it sparks off demands amplification, rationalisation, and the argument of prose. Hugh MacDiarmid's lyrical poems, written in the 1920s and the early 1930s, had that quality. They were true poems, incapable of jingo, and they gave us something that may be described as a definably Scottish insight into universal experiences and values. Thus for a Scot they rang peculiarly true, and so, apart from anything else, they refreshed and deepened our sense of our own particularity. That to many of us was in itself something of a renaissance.

It was in 1928 that, supported by Compton Mackenzie and Hugh MacDiarmid, Cunninghame Graham, standing as a Nationalist, very nearly defeated Stanley Baldwin in the Glasgow University Rectorial. Three years later Compton Mackenzie was himself elected. Few if any enthusiasts would then have predicted how long it was to be before the National Party was to register other electoral successes, but its launching was significant to our background of the Thirties.

At this point I must take stock. I have been asked to contribute to this memorial volume to Hector MacIver an essay on the Scottish literary scene in the 1930s. Yet I have to confess that my interests are not nearly so determinedly literary as those of many whom I know, and of some whom I admire. I could never have given a class of boys at once the depth and the sweep of literary appreciation that Hector MacIver could, even had I had his outstanding gifts as a teacher. My tastes are eclectic. Certain writings and artefacts have affected me profoundly, opened my eyes, enriched my experience, renewed hope or shamed me for my lack of it. Others whose intrinsic merits I would willingly concede have left me unmoved. I cannot claim to be a serious literary critic: certainly not an academic one, able to compare and tabulate, evaluate and formidably denigrate. Furthermore I have neither a good memory nor have I kept diaries or notes, or even many books or publications. So the best I can do is to become merely autobiographical, recording what I can remember as a writer during the Thirties: years which, since I was born in 1910, carried me neatly through the twenties to the thirties of my own age.

The strength of my feeling that Scotland was my home doubtless derived from my having spent my first five formative years very happily in Galloway, with sorties to Edinburgh and Lanark, before going south to live in Middlesex. Life for me there was never so good as it had been before. Later, holidays and one year of schooling in Scotland, contrasting with some miserable schooling in England, increased my partiality for my homeland, and I was always conscious of a difference of temperament between my own family and our southern neighbours.

About the time when I first went to work in London, Moray Maclaren's cheerful travelogue *Return to Scotland* came out. T. S. Eliot, who encouraged me in some thin times by giving me books to review for the *Criterion*, was in no confusion about the distinctive identity of the Scots. He lent me two small books which in their different ways reflected the Renaissance idea. One was George Malcolm Thomson's *Caledonia*, statistical and practical; the other, more inspiriting and poetic, John R. Allan's *New Song to the Lord*. It seemed to me that things were happening in Scotland and in 1932 I made my return, personally prospectless and penniless but full of high hopes in a Cause.

I think I was quite ready, at 22, to man the barricades, and I remember my disappointment when I first made the journey from Edinburgh to Glasgow and met the leaders of the SNP. Glasgow at that time was still firmly bowler-hatted. I rather think there was a special Glasgow bowler-hat, distinctive in its relationship of brim to bowl. It was certainly not worn jauntily, and worn soberly, the bowler gives men a sad, dull appearance, hard to identify with the plumed helmets that the romantic mind associates with a brave cause. The grave, aspiring politicians donned their bowlers and took me out to coffee in an oppressively over-oaked coffee-room, where conversation lapsed in mutual discontent. I was more impressed by a visit I paid to Emrys Hughes, the Welsh editor of Tom Johnston's socialist paper, *Forward*. There seemed to be some fire to him. Doubtless more than in prospective Parliamentary candidates, who may feel the need to trim their sails to electoral breezes, a passionate belief in the relevance of what they say is required to keep men editing and filling the pages of papers unsubsidised and of small and precarious circulation. In Edinburgh the staff of the *Freeman* was likewise passionately committed to keeping its starkly printed pages appearing regularly every week.

The *Freeman* was edited from India Buildings, now cherished as a fine example of Victorian commercial building but then dusty and down-at-heel. Robin Black was the editor, a little dark man with an impressive limp who sat in an inner sanctum while Christopher Grieve, George Dott and T. D. MacDonald

73

wrote—when they were not arguing with or expatiating to all comers—in an ante-room. The genial George Dott had a headful of facts and figures. The *Freeman* was as much concerned to propagate the Douglas Social Credit system as Nationalism. I was no stranger to Social Credit ideas, since my father was an enthusiast. Grieve, however, was enthusing over communism. His *Hymns to Lenin* appeared at this time. So did Eliot's *Ash-Wednesday* which I found much more sympathetic. It seemed to me poetry and politics inevitably made bad bedfellows: whereas religion as the negation of materialism was the very proof of poetry.

In London I had been writing what I intended as a pamphlet. Called 'Balmorality', it was a protest against various Victoriana, tartan terrorism and suchlike, and a rather severe diatribe against the Church of Scotland. David Cleghorn Thomson, then head of the BBC in Scotland, was engaged, under the impact of the first triumph of the SNP, in compiling a symposium which he called *Scotland in Search of Her Youth* (portentous perhaps, but it suited the mood of the day), and 'Balmorality' was included in that.

Re-opening this long-forgotten volume, I find inevitably that much of it has dated (but the worst fault of my own contribution lies in its sheer ignorance of Scottish history: although I might have been left just as ignorant had I been educated entirely in Scotland). Moray MacLaren's essay, 'Scottish Delight', still reads entertainingly, and the transcript of Compton Mackenzie's Rectorial address stands up well to the passage of time. Concerning 'Letters' there were relatively few illusions. James Bridie wrote caustically: 'Scots novelists, poets, dramatists have been rapidly detected, hopefully encouraged, fed on jam and judicious advice, bought, ballyhooed, broadcasted, had their temperatures taken two-hourly and have flickered and failed. They lie in a row parallel with the Horizontal School of British Heavyweight Boxing. You must excuse me from writing about them until they show the stamina and consistency of output of Scots engineers, or pathologists or philosophers or chemists.' Neil Gunn saw possible improvement as dependent upon wider issues: 'Scotland cannot go in quest of her youth without adequate transport. In fact, you might take Transport as a symbol for the whole body politic and easily prove that we need expect no literature of any consequence until the national joints begin to creak consciously and properly. History would bear you out, even if the literary critics would bear you down.'

Still surviving at this time was the *Scots Observer*, successor to that originally edited by W. E. Henley in days when my grandmother was a regular contributor. Latterly it had been edited by William Power, a universally benevolent man who continued to the end of his days to publicise without discrimination every Scot who wielded any sort of professional pen. (Unkind critics said the rowth of names he constantly listed contributed materially to his linage—but his benevolence was unquestionable.) Morison, the owner of the paper, was its last editor, and immediately before its demise brought off a distinguished double in serialising John R. Allan's *Farmer's Boy* and Colin Walkinshaw's *Scots Tragedy*, both of which quickly reappeared in book form. John Allan's autobiographical sketch gives a memorable picture of boyhood on an Aberdeenshire farm: he contracted to write it while in a state of euphoria after my wedding-feast—this was in 1934. Colin Walkinshaw, whose identity long remained a matter of speculation, wrote in *Scots Tragedy* a brilliant brief history of Scotland. Although in the decay of Scottish publishing it remained far too long out of print, its influence was deep, if not as wide as it should have been. *Scots Tragedy* deserves the epithet seminal, for in it Scotland is viewed in true context, the European one: something that had hardly been done since the Union, after which Scottish historians began to bend the lines of history so that they should meet satisfactorily in the submergence of Scotland in the 1707 creation 'Great Britain', cornerstone of Empire, this being both inevitable and a good thing. They hardly noticed that English historians were under no such illusions about the destiny of their country but took the Union in their stride as implying no diminution of England.

Yet to see Scotland as a unit of Europe is alone realistic, since this is a geographical fact, whereas her relationship with England under the Union is only a political expedient that could change in a way that geography does not: while the British Empire has, more quickly than anyone could have supposed in the 1930s, evaporated. Indeed, in face of certain of the régimes that have replaced it, the fierce strictures that we used to pass upon the poor old Empire in those days, endorsing the withering indictments of Bernard Shaw, seem rather over-done. Yet the change was inevitable: although I suppose that in Britain the underlying notion of history built up by 19th-century writers, by which civilisation was seen as reaching its apotheosis in the British Empire, have blinded our peoples to many realities. *Scots Tragedy* was certainly a much more important book than so many others of this period that gained wider publicity and circulation at the time: not unnaturally, most proved as transient as the leaves that blow away with the autumn winds.

1934 brought the annual PEN Conference to Edinburgh. This I remember chiefly for the first meeting that I and my wife Ann —herself an Orcadian and daughter of a close schoolfriend of his—had with Edwin and Willa Muir. In every way Muir was the antithesis of MacDiarmid, except insofar as each was physically small but great in achievement. MacDiarmid developed as a poet relatively early in life with a lyricism such as had scarcely been known in Scotland since the days of Burns. This vein seemed worked out quite abruptly some time during the Thirties. It is, I believe, argued that the average effective period during which the peculiar delicate balance between intuition and intellect that makes the true lyric poet is sustained is 15 years, and I suspect that MacDiarmid's poetic phase matches up pretty well with this.

Contrariwise, Muir seemed to have no equivalent flair. His approach was entirely different—a long, deliberate apprenticeship to poetry that only quite late in his career reached its peak in a few lovely poems. But unlike MacDiarmid, whose prose was never more than a forceful journalese, Muir was an outstanding critic, able to make wise, generous but discriminating assessments over an extraordinarily wide range of literature. Perhaps, morever, he will be remembered best for one prose work that I think stands out from all the books being written in Scotland at the time, the autobiography that appeared originally at the very beginning of the war, and was brought to its splendid conclusion in the post-war years.

MacDiarmid and Muir were two writers of the Renaissance whose best work could be deeply appreciated (despite the former's use of Scots) outside their own country. They succeeded in 'drawing the universal out of the particular': as ever, this was done by an intensive understanding of their own backgrounds, not (although MacDiarmid in his later writings tried to achieve it that way) by trying to be cosmopolitan and fashionable. Frank O'Connor said to me once that MacDiarmid should have been to Scotland what Yeats had been to Ireland. When I quoted this to Eliot, he observed that MacDiarmid had something Yeats never had: with which I would agree, but of course what O'Connor had meant was that MacDiarmid should have been a leader, the inspiration of younger writers. This, for all his personal charm, MacDiarmid could not be: he was too wayward, without firm intellectual grasp, and too easily influenced by undiscriminating flattery. It was a pity that MacDiarmid's cantankerousness, and probably the influence of foolish ones, made a permanent rift between him and Muir.

Of Muir's principal work I was interested to hear a distinguished American professor, Barry Ulanov, describe it as the finest autobiography of the century, especially as Ulanov, born of a Russian-Jewish family, shared none of Muir's background. (Incidentally, a suggestion for some American graduate in search of a recondite theme for a thesis might be the Orcadian Influence on American Literature: both Herman Melville and Washington Irving had Orcadian fathers, and Robert Frost's mother, although born in Leith, was of Orkney parentage, as Muir discovered when they met in America.)

Of the 1934 PEN Conference occasions, I remember best the banquet. With Cunninghame Graham presiding, the menu, I think, arranged by Moray MacLaren, it was an evening that warmed to splendid bonhomie. Three people said to me at different points: 'You Scots—you are not like the English, you are like us!' One was Austrian, one Norwegian, and the third French, and it seemed to me that it could only mean that the English were the most *different* people in Europe: doubtless an accident of history rather than race.

But most of that summer of 1934 we spent at home in our cottage in the hills near Peebles. Ann was writing the first of her children's books. I was editing *Scottish Country* for my publisher, Wishart, who had just brought out *English Country* under the editorship of H. E. Bates. *Scottish Country* did not do as well as, looking at it again after many years, I think it deserved to. It contains some well-shaped essays on different parts of the country by writers who had something to say, who generally knew their chosen countryside intimately, and whose names represent a fair cross-section of our literary Thirties. They ranged from a learned essay on Lothian by old Dr Mackay Mackenzie, an admirable historian who never got all his amassed lore onto paper, to the highly idiosyncratic piece, with its many quotations from sources relevant and irrelevant, written by Hugh MacDiarmid about the Shetlands where he was then living. Neil Gunn wrote of his own Caithness and Sutherland, and Eric Linklater of his native Orkneys. James Fergusson wrote a scholarly essay about Ayrshire, and his brother Bernard more personal reminiscences of Galloway. James Whyte, the American who ran a bookshop in St Andrews and edited *The Modern Scot*, the current cultural periodical, contributed the essay on Fife, which he shot around in a car that could, and did, travel at 100 miles an hour. John R. Allan wrote with bitter-sweet affection of the North-East, 'the cold shoulder of Scotland'. Campbell Nairne wrote on Perthshire and Colin Walkinshaw (his identity still unknown to me) on the Borders. Quite one of the best of the essays was Hector MacIver's piece on the Outer Isles. It seemed to me full of exciting promise and I took it for granted that we should see much more of his writing. I suppose in those days when literary achievement seemed so desirable and so very important, it would have seemed something like tragedy to me to have known that this essay was in fact to be one of the few things he can ever have published. Now it is easier to understand relative values and to appreciate that Hector's talents found their fulfilment differently.

Hector, Robert Garioch and others used to come out from Edinburgh to visit us in Peeblesshire, and for a time T. D. Mac-Donald lived with us. He had published his first novel. *The Albanach*, under his pseudonym Fiona MacColla, and was at work on a more mature book, his impressive novel of the Highland clearances, *And the Cock Crew*, although it was some years before it was to see publication. Some halcyon days ended when Ann took ill and we had to leave our cottage, since it was damp. However, after she had been operated on and convalesced, we made a new home nearby, over the hill in the valley of the Tweed.

Around that time Hugh MacDiarmid and Leslie Mitchell
78

collaborated in a piece of flyting. I forget even its title. I thought it very bad at the time, and a recent rereading of Mitchell's contributions, now republished in a collection of fugitive pieces, endorsed that opinion. Even my own knowledge of Scottish history, as evident in 'Balmorality', compared favourably with the wanton ignorance shown by Leslie Mitchell from his vantage-point in Welwyn Garden City. It was, of course, as Lewis Grassic Gibbon that Mitchell did much of his best work: but the amazing quantity of his output seemed to me more remarkable than most of its quality.

After the demise of *The Modern Scot* various publications sprang up and died down. The *Scots Standard* and *Outlook* were two of them, and MacDiarmid must have been involved in several that had even briefer lives. Moray MacLaren having been refused right of succession as head of the BBC in Scotland on religious grounds, Scottish broadcasting entered upon the long winter of its mediocrity during which practically every bright member of the staff, such as Robert Kemp and Moultrie Kelsall, found it impossible to remain with it. This, especially since broadcasting was taking over many of the functions of the press, was a major misfortune. The importance of the entrepreneur who presents works to the public can hardly be overrated. Good editors, publishers, theatrical producers, even art dealers, are the very reason for the existence of much that is best. I know of many writers and potential speakers who could have made the Scottish Region outstandingly good—as indeed it should have been—instead of the dullest and deadliest of all the Regions, a position it sustained for some 30 ignominious years.

Visiting Ireland with Robin Johnston-Stewart, we formed the idea of running a joint Scottish-Irish quarterly, hoping that some of the better Irishmen might set a standard and serve as a stimulus for our own writers. After the usual inevitable delays in getting launched, the impact of the first issue of the *New Alliance*, which appeared in the autumn of 1939, was somewhat diminished by the outbreak of war.

The Irish contributors to that first issue included Frank O'Connor, F. R. Higgins and Michael Burke. Colm Brogan wrote on the Irish in Scotland, whose latter-day immigration, it may be recalled, was still the object of considerable suspicion and resentment 30 years ago. Hugh MacDiarmid contributed four of what must have been amongst the last poems written in his earlier poetic vein. Edwin Muir had a poem full of apprehension of the days to come. Amongst the short stories we printed was a sensitive sketch of childhood by Morley Jamieson, then a young writer and one whose work, had Scottish publishing not been declining into the moribund condition it occupies today, would long since have appeared in book form. Hector MacIver reviewed a book of mine in an unsigned review. We generally did print our reviews unsigned, not from any fear of reprisals from wounded authors but simply out of a dislike for the kind of reviewer whose concern is not so much with the book or play he is supposed to be reviewing than with parading his own smartness.

We also reproduced some paintings by W. G. Gillies. Too small and in black-and-white, they did his work no credit: we were wiser in later issues when we used line-drawings by Gillies, Jack Yeats and Aleksander Zyw. In painting, Gillies was to me what MacDiarmid was in poetry: re-interpreting some part of the Scottish scene for me, making me more aware of, and so enriching, the life around me. Sickness in the arts often derives from their being treated as goddesses, instead of the handmaids which is all they are. The arts should be servants to our living: I see art for art's sake as a sorry heresy of decadence, cultivated when people have grown timid and distrustful of vitality, as emasculating in its current shock tactics as in the opulent mannerisms of the 1890s. The effort to be cosmopolitan is the work of barren minds. For we only really know a little corner of the world (as indeed of ourselves); yet if men can explore and expound that validly, they achieve a universality impossible to those whose artistic effort is styled to fashions. Paradoxically, it is just because Dostoevsky is intensely Russian, Proust intensely French, Duccio intensely Italian—even specifically Sienese—that they can speak to us in our own language. Charity, which begins at home, is a major element in all true artistic effort: it is part of the responsibility of any artist, exalted or lowly, to interpret for his own countrymen something of their home and its people.

Gillies brought an innocent eye—quickened but not betrayed by French influence—to both the Highland and Lowland scenes.

4. *Hugh MacDiarmid outside his cottage at Candymill near Biggar*

5. *Muriel Spark*

Where many predecessors had seen the Highlands as a series of mountains to be rendered by mountains of paint, Gillies appreciated that mountains are in themselves intractable material, best left to such formalising media as the aquatints of the early 19th century: he recognised the beauty and the essence of the Highlands as lying in such things as the little cultivated strips of crofters' fields, or a conglomeration of cottages with red-rusted corrugated-iron steading-roofs dotted over a knobbly, uncomplying landscape. If he saw the mountains, he saw them as a delicate distant detail far back from a tumble of gnarled rocks on the shore, in the middle distance the sea running blue-green and purple over white sand and red weed. In the Lowlands Gillies recaptured the small mystery of winding by-roads flanked by sensuously stretching beech limbs or austerely plumed pines. He revealed the innate beauty of the mess of mud and tangled sodden herbage of a winter field. Gillies and his more abstract contemporary, Johnnie Maxwell, were painters of a stature to give us a new look at our country's face. At the beginning of the war Gillies bought our house in the Midlothian village of Temple, whither Hector MacIver had first come on visits to us and where he and his wife later spent the last years of his life, with Gillies as their congenial friend and neighbour.

Scotland has had to depend too long upon the *goût Anglais* for what has been considered publishable. Towards the doomful end of the Thirties my wife Ann wrote the last and best of her children's books (and how influential a good children's book can be!), *Auntie Robbo*. Her London publisher rejected it as 'too Scottish', and there was no likely Scottish publisher to whom she could go, so she sent it to America where it was at once published by the Viking Press. Nonetheless it was 20 years before I found a publisher for it in Britain, since when it has been acclaimed a children's classic, has been translated into German and Danish, and is in constant demand as a Penguin paperback. Take-over bids have now reduced Scottish publishing to a vacuum that would be insufferable in any other country with a five-million literate population.

The history of the *New Alliance* belongs to the Forties rather than the Thirties. We kept it going as a bi-monthly throughout the war years. Gradually much of the Irish end faded out as the war cut us off from contacts there, but we published many new Scottish writers: Sydney Goodsir Smith, Sorley MacLean Douglas Young, George Campbell Hay, Elspeth Dryer, Dorothy Haynes amongst them. In 1945 we bowed ourselves out by bequeathing the *New Alliance* along with a new title, the *Scots Review*, to the care of Wilfred Taylor, Robert Kemp, David MacEwen and others.

The *New Alliance* readership, if never large, was appreciative, and we survived longer than any comparable production. We did not confine ourselves to being artsy, which I think is a mistake that has afflicted a number of our successors of the Fifties and Sixties: we had a point of view and a wider concern. This owed much to J. M. Reid, who emerged from the alias Colin Walkinshaw and who was then editor of the Glasgow daily paper, the *Bulletin*. He was in a position to be well-informed, and, with his historical sense and training, was very much better able to assess current affairs throughout the war years than the vast majority of commentators of the time. He could give expression to this more freely in our pages than was always possible elsewhere. Years later a shrewd American writer, Dr Russell Kirk, after reading the files of the *New Alliance*, commented that very few journals appearing during the war had shown such prophetic insight as to the course of events.

The Scottish Renaissance that we talked of in the Thirties doubtless never fulfilled the aspirations we had for it, and while in 1945 we thought parturition might continue, it began to seem as though we had fostered a stillbirth. For a time the whole Scottish movement seemed dead. As Hector bitterly remarked at that time, efforts in the Nationalist cause were 'like farting against a hurricane'. But today it is easier to see the thought and aspirations of the Thirties in their place, as part effect, part cause, of a process of change that could be the hope and inspiration of a post-British Scotland, a Scotland that is once again European.

# 6

## Strangers

### by Robert Taubman

Hector MacIver came to teach at the Royal High School of
Edinburgh in 1934 straight from College. It was a temporary
job, there weren't many jobs going, and when he left, as I
learned afterwards, it was with the idea of working on a sheep-
farm. He didn't look like a new master. Even to me—not long
arrived from England and still bewildered—he stood out among
High School masters as simply not belonging there at all. The
privileged eccentricity of schoolmasters was a different thing—
and much later on Hector let himself acquire it; he *became* a
schoolmaster; but at that time he was not merely new to the
profession, he was not long off the boat from the Isle of Lewis.
He had in fact a remarkable gift for teaching, but even in school
this didn't seem entirely relevant. It didn't matter compared
with what he was, a complete and distinct person, strange to all
of us in many ways—the Highland voice and lack of a classroom manner—but mainly in his very confidence that there *was*
a difference: between his background and ours, between him
and each of us. He struck us, inevitably, as a man rather than
a schoolmaster, as if the fact that he was a stranger, almost a
foreigner, made it easier to see a man there instead of what we
usually saw, the teacher and the system.

He set us to write 'an experiment in autobiography'—not the
usual sort of essay—and writing it I seemed strange to myself,
defined for the first time against someone else. Maybe it was also
one of the moments when one grows up suddenly, for I felt,
handing it over, that this put us on equal terms. It was a sense
of entering an adult relationship, which is what he established with a number of us during that term, and kept up afterwards. In the fourth form the curriculum changed from 'Il

83

Penseroso' to 'Flannan Isle', *Twenty Years A-Growing* and the Ballads:

> I hae dream'd a dreary dream
> Beyond the Isle of Skye;
> I saw a dead man win a fight
> And I think that man was I.

Many of us were to remember Hector for the stories of ghosts and shipwrecks that went along with these texts. But he was also teaching English from an angle that aligned some of its masterpieces with his own interests. Wordsworth's 'Highland Reaper' *was* English poetry for him, just as *Macbeth*, then and always, was *his* play.

The school was a stone building on descending levels of the Calton Hill: all portico and pediment, with stone walls that wound inward and staircases as in a castle, rising or descending to classrooms without giving anywhere the impression of reaching an interior—as if there were, among all the levels, stonework, stairs, passages, a real interior still to be found.

It was a place of conscious tradition, unlike the South-of-England school I came from, but not amenity—tradition took the form of a good deal of antiquarianism and discomfort. The lavatories in the 'dungeons', where boys went to smoke, were impenetrable, for any purpose, if one wasn't used to this sort of rigour. I found the boys in my form remarkable for their long trousers, experience with girls, independence and silence. They were more mature than English boys, but in another direction than any maturity took in an English school, with its cameraderie of boys and masters and certain at least conversational graces. Here boys were united against the masters—remote men, aspects of the tradition, later to be recognised among their counterparts in the pages of Henry Cockburn and Alexander Carlyle. But among the boys themselves there was perfect equality. In an unplanned, pre-Comprehensive way, middle- and working-class, toughs and scholars, were all one (though not so in the official view—there was discrimination all right against those who didn't do enough Latin and Greek to avoid having to do science). My English snobberies about tidiness or accent or what parents 'did' weren't, I think, particularly resented—they were just not understood.

We were both strangers there, which may have helped to bring us together. Hector could make that sort of unexpected conjunction, as one found in class. Celtic writers were a link with modern ones: after O'Flaherty and Neil Gunn's *Morning Tide*, Herbert Read and Ezra Pound. Soon he got onto Joyce's *Portrait of the Artist* and the first Dylan Thomas. Hector changes for me, at this stage, from the Highland stranger to the figure of the Thirties I got to know, green-paper-bound *Ulysses* under his arm, who sent postcards of Franz Marc horses and the Van Gogh portrait of a young man (a portrait he resembled).

One of these conjunctions was in the First World War ethos that still counted for much in the Thirties. I had vaguely apprehended it in England, in Armistice Day ceremonies and schoolboy stories. The war was more immediate to Hector, who had his own memories of it and had lost a brother. The first poem he gave us to learn in the fourth form was Wilfred Owen's 'Anthem for Doomed Youth', and the first book he lent me was Sassoon's *Memoirs of an Infantry Officer*. I was more remote from the war, but recognised the ethos—it was essentially English. And it was common ground for us to meet on. Its spokesmen included T. E. Lawrence and later, in an honorary way, Richard Hillary—for it lingered on, a far more potent expression of English bourgeois attitudes and nostalgias than anything the Thirties came up with, until well into the next war. And in the same vein, confirming an oddly English propensity, there was Hector's love of Housman, spring and cherry-trees. Many roads out of Edinburgh where Housman was recited on our walks now seem as deep in cherry-trees as Ludlow, and stuck fast in the year of the Silver Jubilee.

Hector was by then at another school, holding his job precariously. On these walks we met contemporaries of his out walking because they were unemployed; some had never had a job. At school we were all poor; I knew no one who owned a car; and my family got by on 30 shillings a week. Yet time spent with Hector was full of extravagances—taking taxis, buying books, leaving behind uneaten sandwiches in tea-shops. I was growing up, but that hadn't much effect on my sense of values. The thick, well-margined *New Statesman* meant the world not just of intelligence but of ease and luxury. The tea-shops were solid, plushy and hushed (they no longer are): these were the

'Cranston's and Crawford's' of Auden's poem from the film *Night Mail*, printed by the GPO; Hector brought along a copy from the post office. It wasn't unemployment or talk of fascism that I noticed, but comforts and assurances, and intrusions of new interests. Hard-talking students passed us on the road to the Pentland Hills, and the word 'Nietzsche' floated back. Among other extravagances, Hector implanted in me the idea of going to the university. And he himself was at his most open and inquiring. When we met it was to go to something new to both of us—Greta Garbo or the Markova-Dolin ballet or a Mosley demonstration. He was even open to my attempts to educate *him*. In return for his efforts to bring me round to Gaelic literature I pressed on him *Raffles* as a guide to cricket and English manners, and at a later stage *The Magic Mountain*, writing out an English translation of its many passages in French (he wasn't good at cricket or French). But I never knew if he read any of the books I lent him.

Then and for some years afterwards he wore a blue serge suit, no doubt his only one: a bit frayed and shiny, and tight at the seams as if he had grown since it was bought. Schoolmasters were usually more dressy, or wore sports-jackets and flannels. A boy coming to Edinburgh to study would buy such a suit— his first suit—or to start work in an Edinburgh lawyer's office; or it would do for someone off a deep-sea trawler, which is more what Hector looked like. It strikes me now as a suit that made no claim on a class in society, but no concessions either.

I was surprised that he wanted to buy George Malcolm Thomson's *Scotland—That Distressed Area* or to find him reading Orwell's *The Road to Wigan Pier*. Politics had not been mentioned at school. It didn't take long to discover that he was vaguely socialist and a Scottish Nationalist; but it took me longer to realise what any of this meant. Brought up on the *Daily Mail*, about all I knew was that we lived under Baldwin's 'National Government', and I supposed that was all right: so when one day Hector declared I ought to be a nationalist I said I was one. I didn't understand why he hadn't expected this answer. I had never heard of Scottish Nationalism.

His convictions about nationalism were in fact so much a part of him that they never seemed like what I recognised in other people as their 'politics'. And nationalism of his kind could encompass a large measure of contempt. An obsessional Irishman like James Joyce could hate his country rather more than he loved it; and I see Hector on his side, not with the town baillies, the politicians and committee-men, or whoever would become the ruling class of an independent Scotland. From where we stood, Scotland offered no view of what it might be; but it was obvious what it was, and this made it hard to imagine any aspiration of which the tone wasn't set by an education committee.

What Hector felt about the Outer Isles was quite different— an acceptance and complete confidence that I never noticed when anyone spoke about Scotland. His basic conviction, which gave a liberating sense to nationalism, was that the people of the Highlands and Islands were capable of working out their own destiny. There was a joke figure in the story—Lord Lever-hulme, the soap manufacturer, who had tried to commercialise the Isle of Lewis in the Twenties and been defeated by the islanders. But there was also an immediate enemy, the promoters of the hydro-electric power schemes of the Thirties. One heard of plans to blow up dams and power-lines in the Highlands. Peter Thomsen, a master at the High School—a mild, bearded figure of Scandinavian origin, whom one thought of as a foreigner because of his looks and his way of caring about unexpected things—wrote a pamphlet against pylons in the glens; though Thomsen was a aesthete and cared mainly about the look of them.

In an important sense, however, Hector's concern was cultural too. He was against imposed solutions of the Highland problem, because it wasn't economics or politics but the people and their traditions that he cared about. His talk was full of references to the working life of the people—getting in a crop, mending the roof, stacking the peats—and it was a step from this to the evictions, the depopulation of the glens, and the failure of any Westminster government to understand the problem. It was also, of course, only a step to socialism, which had less to do with Marx or Attlee than with ingrained distrust of owners and landlords. If there was much I couldn't judge, I never doubted the intimate connection between what Hector thought and real experience. I was amazed one night at Fort William with his cousin Isaac MacIver—a more aggressive socialist and a promoter of the Ben Nevis hydro-electric scheme—to hear Hector and all his views discounted as romantic.

The Thirties are far enough off to have become mythical—as far off now as we were then from the turn of the century and the Boer War. A girl who waved, cycling past on a road in the Borders—and a girl from Lewis in her Edinburgh digs, reading for an exam with the clock turned to the wall. The same girl or another? Because a lot of memories are fragmentary or un-identifiable, it's partly a private mythology. But even at the time Scotland seemed to provide fit characters for it: learned eccentrics living at the end of drives, and drinkers in back rooms—an underground of scholars and story-tellers. And this matched the more public mythology of the Thirties coming in from London. Louis MacNeice went to the Outer Isles in 1936 under Hector's auspices and wrote *I Crossed the Minch*, a very Thirties view of the scene: crofting and fishing had less part in it than passwords and ultimatums and auguries of war.

This new language was highly seductive, though for reasons that now seem suspect. The time had a tendency to turn minority movements into new Establishments with a new and comfortable feeling of consensus around them. No doubt the most effective was that of the scientists, emerging from the *demi-monde* and starting to assume power. It was something like that with the poets—Auden, MacNeice and others—because one thought of them as a group, an in-group at that, and because they used the language of power to defend the right, as one saw it—a new language of liberals-come-to-power. The ease of their progress, their very success, made them attractive. That somewhat sinister intimation of success came later to attach to innovation for its own sake, success became its own standard and power more than ever synonymous with right—much later, but all this was com-ing to birth in the Thirties.

MacNeice gave us a mythology—'exposure of the lie', 'the need to hold the ditch'—in which the gesture counted for more than the meaning, though it was a meaning one subscribed to with a sense almost of liberation. And he made a link between Hampstead and Barra, with what seemed then a fine atmos-pheric feeling for place, and now seems only a feeling for a moment in time—*our* time and the way in which we, thoroughly deceived, liked to think of it.

He was very dark, hidalgo-looking, 30-years-old, on his way to Barra: discussing time-tables in the Roxburghe Hotel in Edinburgh; and hardly taking his eyes off the girl who was going with him—though he did turn them on me, with eyebrows raised in a silent stare: perhaps to ask what I wanted to drink, or, as it looked to me, what the hell I was doing there at all.

I was taken to a house in the New Town to meet John Duncan: the ageing, distinguished painter of the 'Celtic Renaissance', a counterpart of the writer Fiona Macleod. This movement, like William Morris's, had sometimes managed a strange conjunction of the dreamy and practical, as in Patrick Geddes with whom Duncan worked. But his painting was of the dreamy kind; the walls were hung with Celtic fantasies in a Pre-Raphaelite manner. He regretted their lack of spontaneity; he thought painting a less direct art than literature. Hector argued that the Celtic elaboration in Yeats was akin to his painting. Only the young Yeats, the painter said. He denied there was any 'poetry' in the later Yeats. Hector quoted the six lines of 'Oil and Blood' from *The Winding Stair*: 'In tombs of gold and lapis lazuli . . .' It wasn't seemingly very different from the paintings on the wall; yet it's a violent poem. The oil and blood were too 'direct' for the old painter, who shivered with disgust.

Everyone who was taught poetry by Hector will have his own account of what he learned. For me it was, above all, 'pure poetry'—a Thirties thing, though remote from the direction poetry was actually taking. There wasn't much of it, only single lines or verses: 'Childe Roland to the dark tower came' and 'A widow bird sate mourning for her mate', with some modern approximations:

> But once upon a time
> The oak-leaves and the wild boars
> Antonio Antonio
> The old wound is bleeding.

It was a taste that easily turned to indulgence. I don't remember that he was ever indulgent about prose. He didn't use books as a refuge, and can't be imagined with a detective story. Orwell yes, Priestley no—he made it his task to wean me from popular fiction, which I took to be realistic, and teach me that realism could be thoughtful and imaginative. He was a realist himself in areas where the educated line was still, in those days, romantic—about Scottish literature, for instance. He wrote stories (for little magazines that are now untraceable) that were as close to the life of the Western Isles as he could get. It was the life of a pre-industrial, imaginative people—it gave him different subjects from those of English realists, and he thought them better subjects; but it was nothing strange about them, only their ordinary and obvious interest, that he wanted to establish.

The hell-fire sermon in *A Portrait of the Artist as a Young Man* was often quoted—it was a link between the Jesuits and his own Calvinist island. He had a certain notoriety at home as an enemy of the Kirk; but he was susceptible to the splendours and spleen of the Gaelic pulpit and the language of damnation, and when a word like 'fornication' appeared in his stories it didn't look stark so much as theological. He took to visiting Catholic churches in Edinburgh, but I think only out of secular piety—he never forgot that it was the Catholic islands which had preserved the old pagan Gaelic songs and stories. He was a theist of a kind. He didn't make an issue of the existence of fairies—though that had the authority of Yeats—but he believed they were symbols of something else; and considered he couldn't know anyone who didn't acknowledge a 'spiritual background' to life.

How to live in a city, where to fit in—since a city offers choices, and a choice once made changes the way one sees oneself—isn't just a matter of address but of commitment. Hector had different styles of living. He was guest or lodger with Harvey Wood, Professor W. J. Watson and Sir Herbert Grierson, all of Edinburgh University; and this seemed to me his natural role. He defined himself in it without deference to the background, but the background had an austere interest of its own; and I suppose that the life of scholarship, dour as it may be in Scotland, was something Hector never lost a respect for. At other times he had hide-outs or digs in some seedy parts of Edinburgh, lived in a back room like a student and received his friends in pubs. Much later, when he married and settled at

Temple and for the first time seemed not to be living out of a suitcase or a sea-chest, he astonishingly acquired an interest in gardening and furniture: as a young man he hadn't the least regard for *things* of any kind—except books.

In none of his roles, however, did he merge into Edinburgh. He was conscious of being unusual, even distinguished, as a pure Highlander in Edinburgh—both peasant and natural aristocrat. The aristocratic pride in traditions and origins persisted; it was impossible that he should want to change them: which put him at the other end of the scale from the Celt who gets his promotion by making the change—the South-bound émigrés and successful politicians. Success of that kind was of no account; but he had a Celtic regard for nobility, for exceptions; a fellow-feeling for the arrogant Yeats, Cunninghame Graham and Joyce; and he was known to practice the aristocratic art of displeasing, as if enemies and superiors were there for that purpose. There was no natural bourgeois in him between the peasant and aristocrat, which often made him a difficult friend. He stood off from bourgeois habits, not so much as bourgeois but as foreign—'Edinburgh' or English.

Yet Edinburgh was still a city to respond to on his terms. It had a true working class that was far from Anglified or assimilated into the bourgeoisie, and even the latter had some special, redeeming manifestations. Edinburgh was a stronghold of antique Establishments, still articulated as if to serve the functions of a sovereign state, observing formalities of an Austro-Hungarian complexity and disuetude; but not wholly divorced from the life of the city. The middle class had a strong professional nexus: the law, government, education, the arts and the Church were not only learned professions but active and populous. This professional population never looked like just a piece of class structure; it took its character far more from its stiff, principled, eccentric members—and its hard-drinking, bohemian strain. It was a stronghold, but open to democratic ideas if they were not framed as demands but embodied in an individual. Hector was rough, intelligent, subversive, no friend of Establishments, but a native Scot with all the authenticity of a born Gaelic speaker, and he had an eye for character. He was liked and taken up in very different circles, wherever an interest was discovered in common, which had usually to do with the

91

Highlands or the arts: for he had no social conversation, never discussed anything that didn't mean a lot to him, and had only a faint sardonic interest in the rest of the world's business.

Hector didn't befriend one; he made an assumption of equality that was often disconcerting to me, who hugged the conventions and was preoccupied with the problem of how to know a schoolmaster, even how to write to one: for years I had trouble in sending him a postcard. But if I was growing towards him I was also growing away. He could show me and tell me things, but I obstinately wanted to make my own discoveries; and, such as they were, my discoveries were often in a different direction from his.

A year after Louis MacNeice I crossed the Minch and stayed at the house on the west coast of Lewis, where lying in the sun on the island's gneiss, 'the oldest rock in the world', made one feel like a prehistoric animal; and read books of modern poetry. Hector's mother, the activating force of the family, hoped I would one day occupy a Chair—a little stool maybe, Hector said. His father sat by the fire, worn and unresponsive. Hector and I went into the south, his mother's part of the island, and were passed from house to house among seafaring relatives. We ate lobsters in a fishing-boat at night, and walked through Valtos glen to pick up some illicit whisky. From country buses, I watched a landscape with only one dimension, width—the flat sea, the low slopes of moorland, the level lines where peat was cut from peat-bogs—and my mind stretched, grew level and wide, and I felt I now had a style for writing poetry. I came back from Lewis with the background at last filled in, and yet no wiser about Hector; he remained detached from it. I was shown all over his village, but still couldn't picture him as a child. What I noticed was what I wasn't shown. I remember, far better than anything about Lewis in fact, cycling up to Kyle of Lochalsh by myself, the smell of peat-smoke for the first time, and a vivid experience of loneliness before I fell asleep for 12 hours by the road-side. But in this Hector had no place.

Growing apart was also allied to something in the very nature of the Thirties. One lived with the sense of an undisclosed time-limit, expecting at any moment a radical change; and I was young enough to feel glad about this. Unthinkingly, I believed in change. When Hector got his call-up for the Navy I assumed

92

he would welcome it, just as I'd once encouraged him to take a job he was offered in Canada. He was fierce with me, on both occasions, for my lack of feeling for roots and continuity. For him, who resisted change, the war was only an interlude; for me it meant the end of waiting, and the redistribution of energies that had been long expected. We didn't meet easily afterwards. I was right, one does change—but wrong to suppose it does one any good. Or the point is that one changes anyway, not just on account of a new experience. There was less sweet reasonableness after the war, less natural confidence and many more set attitudes: which would probably have happened anyway, but it was the opposite of what I had expected of change.

It always seems that in England friendships are inevitable, part of the décor, a matter of schools, colleges, groups, interests, patterns . . . They're infinitely rarer, more individual, hard-won and precarious, in Scotland. I should have been grateful: for a long time I lived in someone else's life, accepted his ideas and borrowed his friends (no one was more generous in sharing his friends). But in our case a certain opposition was built in from the beginning; we were opposites drawn together; and instead of making the best of this I saw it as an insuperable difficulty.

On our first trip into the Highlands we climbed Ben Lawers, got benighted in the snow and only by luck found our way back to the inn at Fearnan. I hadn't been north of Edinburgh before; yet this was Central Scotland and as much my territory as Hector's. But he wasn't long in discovering that the inn-keeper had some Gaelic; and the deer crossing a shoulder of Ben Lawers set him talking of the depopulation of the glens. Word was sent out, singers gathered for a *ceilidh*. I saw *my* Scotland carried out of reach and another substituted, a more interesting one perhaps, but already I resented being *shown* it. I felt young and rebuffed. Our positions were reversed: it was I who had become a stranger.

The lost chances are what strike me now about this opposition. If Hector hadn't been the first person I thought of as an opposite I might have been readier to appreciate them then. I didn't know that the only trouble with opposites is that they don't easily make themselves available; or that what Hector put in my way wasn't likely to be put there again.

# 7

# Romantic Town

## by Karl Miller

In 1966, not long before he died, I went to visit Hector MacIver in his cottage at Temple, in the countryside south of Edinburgh. His face showed the marks of a taxing illness, but his hopes, his imagination, and the lustre of his talk, were not extinguished. He told me that someone mysterious had been trying to get in touch with him. This someone had called more than once on the telephone, then he had come to Temple; he had not been admitted to the cottage; and the face which had looked in through the window, that winter night in Midlothian, had been black, some unspecified shade or sort of black. Hector was a story-teller—a *seanachaidh*, in Gaelic. This was perhaps the last of all his stories, and one of the most compelling. It was characteristic of his supernatural vein, and it was not a story which the listener would want to pry into or have explained to him. Scottish literature has plenty of black men, come to warn or threaten; there, and in legend, they are often revealed as the Devil—'black as the Earl of Hell's waistcoat' was a simile Hector was fond of. This was certainly a story of foreboding, and of a traditional kind. It was hard to think of it in relation to the hopes that had been expressed for his recovery.

Eighteen years before that, when I was his pupil at the Royal High School of Edinburgh, Hector used to tell stories about the faculty of second sight, which seemed to be an important matter, still, in the Hebrides where he grew up. I discovered that it was possible to be sophisticated and superstitious at the same time: while you could not call him credulous, it was clear he was deeply impressed by these stories. To Lowland school-children, Hector himself came as a revelation: an exile from the Western Isles, from 'the lone shieling of the misty island', he had qualities

of dignity, elegance, eloquence and fantasy that seemed not
only exotic but literally portentous. His courtesy was not unlike
that of the haughty, solicitous Highland chiefs who flank Bon-
nie Prince Charlie in the well-known painting, their plaids
thrown round some grief or grudge, shielding some mystery.
He, too, was a kind of chief: outlandish, imperious, sometimes
insubordinate—perhaps there are no words for such a person
any more. He was like one of the leaders of the Irish rebellion,
those thick-set country men, the Pearses and Connollys celebrated—to Hector's delight—in the poetry of Yeats. He was also
like Othello: redoubtable, inscrutable and shocking in a city
with more proprieties than Venice ever owned, full of reverend
seniors, with a mercantile middle class that had seen better days
and a petty-bourgeoisie given over utterly to primness. He was
a fabulist, as Othello was, and certain of his tales were not dis-
similar; he had his Anthropophagi and even, it turned out later,
his Iagos; it can be said that we loved him for the stories that
he told. In a sense, he was looking at his own reflection in that
window-pane at Temple.

He was a stranger, a man of different temper and breeding,
born to a different language, learned in a literature and song
that were a closed book to Lowlanders. He was 18 before he
saw a train. It may well be that when I was a child, the past was
nearer, and of more consequence, to Lowland people than it was
in England then. Border Ballads were still sung in their houses;
the rosy shade of Robert Burns was an important thing—I
went off to Ayrshire, on holiday from school, and stared in
homage at his farms—and so, even in Edinburgh, was the harvest. But there could be no comparison with the life inherited by
Hector in the Hebrides: he grew up in a great stillness, in a
society which had changed very little in the course of the centuries. He sent a letter once to the Hebrides asking his mother
and brother 12 questions about the history of the MacIvers.
This catechism, and the answers it received, tell a good deal
about the history of the Highlands.

'In what year did Neil MacIver leave Uig?' '1850–59' was the
reply. 'Who were in the boat with him?' 'Is it true that he had
the rafters of his house in the boat?' 'Did he leave Uig as a
result of a Clearance?' 'If he was evicted, what landlord was
responsible?' The patient answer to this last question is moving,

and instructive: 'Sir James Matheson, one of the most humane of Highland landlords, who (I think) was merely in the evicting fashion of the landlords of that period'.

An ancient world survived in him, and he never forgot those past sorrows. Of that world, and of the sea which surrounded it, he wrote:

> From the first window I ever looked through I saw the Atlantic in its vast hollow lying only a short distance from the gable-head of our house in the Hebrides. For some time in my childish imagination it remained as a big pool, very bonny, but only an enlargement of the miniatures in which I slew eels or studied my shadow. But I was growing up in a Gaelic community where children were caught like fishes in a network of sea-legend and sea-superstition that exhilarated and depressed them alternately. There were stories of the sea's rapacity, its fatal influence on men's minds, its uncompromising attitude to those who did business with it, the treasures that lay beyond it and so on. In this atmosphere I soon began to realise that the Atlantic was after all something more than a cold extensive pool: for besides the legends that made such an insidious appeal to the ear, there was some glaring evidence that came within the range of the eye. I remember some beautiful Clydesdale horses that lodged for a night in our stable. They had come across the wintry moor on a New Year's day bearing an eldritch gift—the bodies of sailors who had been drowned in an appalling disaster on the other side of the island. I remember a furious day in the spring when a sloop from a village further down the coast failed to put into her own harbour because of a sudden storm and tried harbour after harbour until the fantastic concourse of women that followed her along the coast were driven to wild despair by what appeared to be the deliberate malice of the wind.

Coming from such a background, Hector was a living reproof to the Nationalist conception that Scotland was racially or ethnically homogeneous and distinct. He was very patriotic, and an enemy of the parochialism to which a regional status has given rise; and he took part in the Nationalist movement when he was young. But he talked less and less about Nationalism during the years I knew him, and never displayed any very

robust belief in the political possibilities, or desirabilities. He
was aware that the one country of Scotland held a mixture of
races, and at least two languages and two cultural traditions,
and he may have felt in the end that if Scotland could contain
the Western Isles, in however casual and improvident a fashion,
then the British Isles could contain Scotland. He was incapable
of indulging in the half-smiling pantomimes of race hatred that
certain Nationalist writers went in for, and made no bones about
the fact of the Scottish diaspora, the dispersal of native talent
through the world. His friends Louis MacNeice and Dylan
Thomas were not despised for living, despite their blood, in
London; and Dylan Thomas was not despised for despising
Welsh Nationalism. Neither of them was treated as if he were
some Celtic spy who had been posted south to poison the wells
of the Spoken Word in Portland Place.

Hector was no rude forefather-figure, who introduced an
elemental or barbaric note into our parsings and declensions;
nor did his enthusiasms show any of the fustiness and sentimentality associated with regional cultures, with the taste for
brooches, tweeds and *ceilidhs*. He was a sophisticated man, in
an Edinburgh that had need of this quality, and like the Highland chiefs in the painting, he had the air of someone who,
though he might not know much about London, was fairly well
acquainted with Paris. In point of fact, he was never very interested in London, and there were times when he behaved as
if America had yet to be discovered. But there was nothing
parochial about this. He may once have been in the habit, as
Louis MacNeice reported, of sending back his lobster to the
counter in Edinburgh's Café Royal 'if he did not think it came
from Lewis'—nevertheless, the world was his oyster.

The truth is he was very free from meanness of any sort. In
spite of his attitude to the Clearances, he relished the hierarchi-
cal, and the smack of dashing hereditary leadership: he had a soft
spot for the apparently very autocratic Marquis of Graham (son
of the Nationalist Duke of Montrose), who captained a destroyer
he served on during the war, and who is now a leading schismatick
in Rhodesia, one of the lords of the secession. Hector was a little
feudal, but he was no Tory and would not have wished to 'support
Rhodesia'. He was no socialist either, when I knew him, though
he retained a radical streak, and there is no political significance

G 97

in the strange bedfellows who appear among MacNeice's bene-
ficiaries in the 'Last Will and Testament' drawn up by Auden and
himself in *Letters from Iceland*:

> Item to Guy Morgan and also Guy
> Burgess and Ben Bonas and Hector MacIver
> And Robert Dunnett and Norman Cameron
> I leave a keg of whisky, the sweet deceiver.

Hector was neither right nor left, and indeed the politics of
industrial societies never really claimed his sympathy. More
than anyone I have known, he was unaffected by class feeling.

After the war he returned to teaching. His life was divided
between the male sodalities of wardroom (and lower deck) and
staffroom. There were occasions, with Mr MacIver treading in
your direction, when the playground felt very like a deck, for
he could be curt as well as antiquely courteous. And there were
occasions, during the rather oppressive hostility which developed
between him and one of his headmasters, when he resembled
Captain Ahab, the Ancient Mariner and other sea-going zealots.
*Sicut arx in colle sita*, sang the Royal High School of its own
magnificent geographical situation (recently and miserably deserted for a site outside the city). Hector's presence made it an
ark as well as an *arx*, which rode the waves as if in pursuit of
that monster, Arthur's Seat, looming like Moby Dick across the
valley of Holyrood.

When I was in the sixth form I was his friend as much as his
pupil, and we edited the school magazine together, *Schola Regia*,
subduing it to the purposes of modern poetry. The verse we
published was 'obscure' (the word was constantly used) and
recklessly metaphorical. It reflected adolescent worries about the
flesh and its mounting demands, and was peopled by beguiling
seal ladies and the like. The more mettlesome or fashionable
of the literary set attempted the latest poetic styles. Auden and
MacNeice had been displaced by the later Eliot, whose reputation was being challenged by that of Dylan Thomas. At about
this time Dylan Thomas distinguished himself in Hector's
library in Regent Terrace, next door to the school, by telling
as many stories as his host. Hector could not go for a walk
in the country, which he liked doing, without being chased by

a bull; put him in a boat and you got an *Odyssey*. But here the *seanachaidh* had met his match. During the evening Dylan Thomas asked Robert Taubman: 'How do you make your money?' This disclosed an ugly side to his famous nature, according to Taubman, who was imperfectly convivial and suspicious of romantic behaviour, and was living on a university grant.

I wrote several slavish poems under the influence of Dylan Thomas, as did other young men, in other places: William McIlvanney's juvenilia, from which he quotes elsewhere in this book, shows that Thomas's example was heeded in Kilmarnock. I also wrote a parody of his early work which may help to give the flavour of these years. They were exciting years. Provincial? The thought that we were provincial never crossed our minds. What were we denied, as boys interested in books, that other boys had access to? What were we missing? The subject-matter of the parody was undoubtedly parochial: the rector of the school had devised a staff code whereby each master was to be known by a set of initials, as if for processing by computer. But what mattered was the style. It was a way of paying my respects to the author of *Eighteen Poems*, to the force that drove my green age.

> Light breaks where there's no staff, where there's no
>     school
> Windy instruction dawns within the skull
> Of boys alone,
> And broken hearts with tickets in their hands
> File into lunch where no staff picks the bones.
>
> We've no more masters left us, only vowels:
> To passwords capped and gowned belong the tawse.
> With vatic howl,
> In the earth like bones our former ways and days
> We bury wept with pickaxes and trowels.
>
> By burning fire and blowing wind we swear
> That there are ciphers no one can decipher,
> While, dressed in signs,
> Throughout the yard a walking alphabet
> Holds forth in class and brings unsettled weather.

The force that on the white palm drives the leather
Drives the white word, that blasts the first-form boy
Destroys the phrase:
The fragmentary clauses end our tether
Which neither soul nor sense can piece together.

The gownless class, the mortarboardless hall,
The rocket landed flaming in the gym,
All these proclaim
The letters that have done this death are writ
Across the sheds in capitals of flame.

Each bitter morning, too, at nine a host
Enters the poor depopulated well—
The wordy ghosts,
Who double-tongued with blackest book and bell
Ring out their own wild consonantal knell.

How can we hope to disemvowel the staff
Or prove such sentences not consonant
With such a school,
Where there's no men but only syllables
And such semantic rages are the rule?

Darkness descends where J and R and G
Profess Maths, English and Geography:
Alas we find
That though in the beginning was the word
The word split up in portions is the end.

What strikes me now about the poem, as much as anything,
is what an old-world school it describes, with its harping on
rules, rockets, blasting rebukes, corporal punishment and
teachers' regalia. The last two lines were scanned by the rector
for blasphemy, so maybe the description was not all that in-
accurate: student protest, certainly, was unimaginable.

Dylan Thomas was shown this and others of my Dylan
Thomas poems. 'The echoes,' he wrote enigmatically to Hector
from Laugharne in July 1949, 'though I cannot place where
they come from, seem to me not unpleasant.' So much for my
slavishness. The anonymous author of the parody 'I would,

myself, take to be a far older boy with a taste for Scotch, though I may be entirely wrong'. He told Hector that he was 'sorry to see no picture of you in charge of any athletic group', and ended with a cameo of the predicaments of his last years: 'My study, atelier, or bard's bothy, roasts on a cliff-edge. My wife is just about to go to the infirmary to have a Thomas. There are not enough of them already. And now I'm going to greet the unseen with some beer.'

Quite often Hector and I would sit most of the night in his library, pasting up the magazine and talking. In fact, it was not his library at all, but that of Sir Herbert Grierson, whose lodger he was and whose pupil he had been at Edinburgh University. That room made a lasting impression on me, with its scholarly editions of 17th-century plays and verse sheltering in the dim, leafy light from the back garden, in a green shade fit for green thoughts; with its engraved triptych of John Donne, as a young man, then an ageing one, then in his coffin, the inscribed volumes from Yeats, Eliot and Chesterton, the swivelling mahogany receptacles and rests which a high bourgeois society had provided for the dictionaries and concordances of its beloved professors.

The relationship between Hector and Sir Herbert was a study. In general, Hector could appear to combine a captain's, even an Ahab's, bearing with the deference of a first officer, but at 12 Regent Terrace Sir Herbert was his captain and he himself played the part of the first officer invariably and with real virtuosity: he was always addressed there, and always spoke of himself, as 'Mr MacIver'. He also liked to cast Sir Herbert in the role of the absent-minded professor—no difficult task. One day he telephoned the house.

'This is Mr MacIver, Sir Herbert.'

'He's not in.'

'But this is Mr MacIver speaking.'

'I'll go and see . . . I told you he wasn't in.'

'Sir Herbert . . .'

'Yes, can I take a message?'

'There's no message, Sir Herbert. I know I'm not in. This is Mr MacIver speaking.'

'Oh good God, so it is. There you are. That's funny. Well, good night, Mr MacIver.'

This, word for word, was one of Hector's shorter stories.

Both men came from the extremities of Scotland, Sir Herbert from the Shetlands, to which he was greatly attached. He used to tell the story of a Shetland barber who greeted the news that Crippen had been refused a reprieve with 'There's nothing the man can do now but wire into religion.' ('To wire into' is a savage Scots version of 'to tuck into'; there is a suggestion of ravenousness, almost of rape.) I have discovered what I regard as a sequel to that story. A few years ago a Glasgow matriarch presented her sons with some whisky that had been distilled on the premises. 'Get wired into that,' she said. 'The following morning,' said the press report, 'they were either blind or dead.' These stories, you could say, convey the extremes of Scottish life.

After working through the night on the magazine I would set out in the dawn to walk home to my village. I used to pause on the Regent Road escarpment and look over the railway line leading out of Waverley Station on the way to London, and across, in the gaining light, at the conglomerate greyness of the storeys and closes of the Royal Mile, 'slatternly tenements,' in Norman MacCaig's words, 'that made a Middle Ages in the sky'. Down below to my left was the Canongate Churchyard and Robert Fergusson's grave, with its headstone erected by Burns to:

> my elder brother in misfortune,
> By far my elder brother in the Muses.

The school motto declared that the muses were of national importance: *musis respublica floret*. On these occasions, there and then in Regent Road, I felt sure that they were flourishing. Hector made it seem so. His devotion to literature, and to his country, made him a male muse, and inspired those who knew him.

Hector was devoted, above all, to the Border Ballads, Shakespeare, the poetry of the Romantics, and that of Yeats. He loved romanticism's great effects, its great lines. Poetry, for him, was very much a matter of lines, lines to quote, lines to conjure with, lines to chalk up on the blackboard, lines you could borrow and adapt—his less attentive writings were full of ravelled oddments of *Macbeth*. Short poems were compact of good lines, as often as not, and could be chalked up on the board in their entirety. Very early in our acquaintance I saw him take his chalk without preamble and inscribe from memory Hugh MacDiarmid's lyric:

> Mars is braw in crammasy,
> Venus in a green silk goun.

For boys who had been taught that their Scots words were reprehensible, this was an astonishing sight.

Short poems were better than long ones, and we were bored by *The English Parnassus: An Anthology Chiefly of Longer Poems*, despite the fact that it had partly been compiled by Sir Herbert, thinking it a mere repository of narratives with a doubly unpromising title. It lacked lines and did not lend itself to quotation. It did not lend itself, either, to the A. E. Housman test for poetry: that's to say, it did not foster emotion, it did not thrill you, making it hard to shave in tranquillity when the flesh rebelled in recollection. Housman was a favourite poet of Hector's, and it was apt that one of his destroyers should have been named the *Ludlow*—another, no less aptly, was called the *Viking Deeps*. The Housman test (spelt out in 1933 in *The Name and Nature of Poetry*) was frequently brought to the notice of downy pupils, who must at times have regarded poetry as a razor's edge affair, of hazardous shaving at sea, with a lyric propped before you, while your destroyer wrestled the Viking deeps and German submarines converged. Housman's call for a poetry that proved itself not only on the pulses but on the capillaries may be ranked among romanticism's more striking effects, and it applied mainly to romantic poetry. Alexander Pope's was altogether less physiological. For Hector the preceptor there were four R's, and the greatest of these was romanticism. In this respect he never changed. His flesh never crawled at the verse of 'the Movement' in England in the Fifties —dry, civic stuff—and he preferred the ballads of the nautical Charles Causley.

I grew to realise that there was an established opposition to romantic values on the part of those who sided with the Modern. Hector was aware of the doubts that had been cast, he knew that a form of classicism was being enjoined in certain quarters,

103

and he was in fact very sympathetic to most of this. He wished there to be a co-existence between the 19th-century and the New, and that was typical of the more or less deliberate adjustment that was made by those who were unwilling to take the revolutionary pretensions of the innovators too literally. While T. S. Eliot brought distress to many who had a high regard for emotion in poetry, his paradoxes about the importance of tradition for the innovator were no doubt reassuring to those of Hector's mind. The 'really new' work of art, Eliot wrote, did not dislodge 'the existing monuments'; ' "classicism" is not an alternative to "romanticism".'

Hector admired Joyce, smuggling a banned first edition of *Ulysses* across the Minch. He admired Yeats more, whose later poetry may well have seemed to him a kind of validation of Modernism. After the war Eliot's authority sent young men reeling into Anglo-Catholicism and engendered large quantities of bitter, broken allusive-contemplative verse. Eliot was a great quoter, and his poetry had that to recommend it. But I don't believe that Hector was ever deeply drawn to it. It smelt of the lamp rather than the razor. I have a feeling that he preferred the work of that other Sir Herbert, who partnered Eliot in the public eye as leading and personifying the *avant-garde* but who also served for some people as the defender of romanticism: Sir Herbert Read.

'I have been blamed for the obscurity of modern poetry,' Sir Herbert Grierson told Hector once, 'because of my edition of Donne.' This edition had done much to create the taste for the Metaphysical poetry of the 17th century, and had endeared him to Eliot. The Metaphysicals were thought by the pioneering sort to be contemporary, to have leapt, as by the magic of metempsychosis, into modern times, to have written modern poetry before the fact. They were thought to afford further proof of the validity of Modernism, and the idea that the metaphysical might be an attribute of the romantic was not entertained except by the unregenerate. If the moderns had friends in Yeats and the two Sir Herberts, this was in itself a reason for befriending them. Hector's passion for Yeats drove him to take tea in a disconsolate hotel where the waiter resembled the poet in his more senatorial aspect. The hotel was just down the road from Regent Terrace, where Yeats used to stay with Grierson.

I can testify to the likeness, and so could the waiter. Did he know, he was asked, whom he resembled? 'Yes,' he replied, 'the Irish poet, William Butler Yeats.' From then on he was known as William Waiter Yeats.

I suppose it is true to say that these competing views of poetry set up a certain tension in Hector, which was evident, for example, in his references to the 'Canadian Boat Song':

> From the lone shieling of the misty island
> Mountains divide us, and the waste of seas—
> Yet still the blood is strong, the heart is Highland,
> And we in dreams behold the Hebrides.

His own heart was Highland, and he was in exile: so you would have expected the poem to appeal to him. It appeals to me: I find it beautiful, cadenced like a good hymn, and none the worse for its rather simple conventionality. It brims with feeling, but is very manly; the objects of that feeling are not in doubt, and may be felt to approximate to Eliot's objective correlatives. It may also be felt to satisfy Eliot's criterion of 'impersonality' by employing a communal 'we' instead of the 19th century's 'I', and by actually being anonymous. In fact, Hector sometimes spoke ill of it, finding it sentimental, a debilitating nostalgic view of the Hebrides, which condoned an attitude of helplessness towards the problems and realities of the place. He could quote from it, but he could be expected to do so drily and sceptically. Yet I suspect that he responded to it nonetheless, strongly and guiltily. The poem, perhaps, was Hector's Achilles' heel: the languorous feelings it had inspired in so many, the emotion that a vulnerable Hector brought to it, and Eliot's strictures on 'emotion', may all have conspired to make it taboo and to induce unconvincing statutory rejections of it.

Hector had chosen the modern, but the choice was not an easy one. He did not favour a rampant, programmatic Modernism which placed its trust in unrelenting experiment and unrelenting unfamiliarity. Familiarity, indeed, was a required element for him: the modern was to be received among the existing monuments. The modern which was also romantic was consequently very welcome. The romantic never lost its fascination for this critic of Scotland's nostalgias, and he was not alone in wanting to save it from the revolutionary ferment. As a vehicle for feelings of exile, estrangement and discontent, it was natural that romanticism should have had a long run in Scotland, given the country's consciousness of subjection and deprivation, and despite what can be seen as the country's complicity in Britain's imperial and industrial undertakings. The longings and nostalgias embodied in the vernacular and in popular literature are notorious. Even the demotic, in Scotland, is romantic. Romanticism continues to fascinate, and enervate, Scots people; it fascinates Sorley MacLean, in this book; it fascinates me, in this essay.

That being the case, Hector was unlikely to resist the dominion of Dylan Thomas, a modern poet who was also, if ever there was one, a romantic. Comic as he was, he was also vatic. He drank himself to death in his bard's bothy; he had an enthralling personality; he told stories, and caused them; he had a consummate negligence and extravagance of manner (belied by the hard facts of his daily application and costiveness). No contemporary poet could be quoted from as he could: he created lines of poetry, and almost seemed to think in terms of single-line units. He wrote letters to Hector which corruscated with lines, tropes and coinages: the only pubs accessible to him in Oxfordshire, he confided, were 'wild with dominoes'. The poetry of Auden and his generation could never face the physiological reckoning as his could. Louis MacNeice was dearer to Hector, but Dylan Thomas was nearer his notion of what a modern poet should be.

Drastic changes in literary expression seemed to be called for, and young people travelled altarwise by owl-light into obscurity and nonsense without too many qualms. The cult of Thomas, in its early stages, yielded the comforts and amenities of a secret society. Obscurity, which could be copied and which demanded certain skills, became the badge and instrument of a sense of superiority; words became passwords; and the already uncertain general audience for poetry can only have been further reduced by this pursuit of the cryptic. It can be argued that Dylan Thomas ran his gift into the ground in the course of furnishing such codes. The elect, moreover, was compromised by the posthumous and promiscuous adoration of Dylan Thomas which ensued: their secret society (to which, it should be said, Hector himself had never strictly belonged) dispersed, or discoded, loftily. After the ravages of the cult there was a necessary period of sackcloth and restraint.

Modernism could be romantic, and it could also be Scottish. Scotland, in fact, produced one of the leading writers of the Modern Movement in Hugh MacDiarmid. His first lyrics came to him at a time when the governing strategies of Modernism were being laid down, and he applied these strategies to the business of being a national poet. One of the Movement's purposes was the renovation of language, and this he set himself to work at, partly for nationalistic reasons. Lallans or Synthetic Scots (an unlucky term, for those inured to synthetic milk and other wartime elixirs) or Plastic Scots (equally unlucky) was no mere flight into dialect: assembled from different periods and different regions of Scotland, the vocabulary was a highly individualistic construction comparable to the vocabulary of *Finnegans Wake*. For that reason alone I think it can be treated as a romantic monument. MacDiarmid is also a romantic by virtue of the relationship between the subject-matter of his shorter poems and that of their folk-song antecedents and of 19th-century European lyric poetry, and by virtue of his aims as a national poet, national poets being an institution of the emergent countries of 19th-century Europe. It is not surprising that, eclectic as he was, he never took to classicism. Classicism did not suit the poetry he had learnt from; it did not suit his politics, being chiefly affiliated to the Right; it did not suit his atheism, being affiliated to Christianity.

His vocabulary was as obscure, and secret, as Dylan Thomas's metaphors were, and the glossaries were pored over by devotees. None of these devotees, however, proved able to wield the vocabulary themselves. Edwin Muir's remark about Scottish writers—'men of sorrow and acquainted with Grieve'—is telling in more ways than one, for MacDiarmid was not only intractable but inimitable, even by himself: we should not make light of the fact that he eventually abandoned Lallans in favour of a discursive English. The early lyrics, and *A Drunk Man Looks at the Thistle*, were for me his best poetry, and still are. In these poems, the terms of ordinary Scots speech are often retained:

> Wunds wi warlds to swing
> Dinna sing sae sweet,

The licht that bends owre a'thing
Is less ta'en up wi't.

And even in the most inimitable, vertiginous, mutinous and
multitudinous of his verse, the accent of ordinary Scots speech
is never impaired by the 'aggrandisements' he used (his own
word for them, in conversation). This was a poetry of genius.
It was romantic. It was Scottish. It was modern. And it was
wholly free from nostalgia.

It is ironic that the Lallans movement, with its dislike of
Kailyard sentimentality, has tended to become confused with
the Kailyard itself. When the Lallans flag first flew, the movement was considered piratically *avant-garde*. MacDiarmid himself plainly had revolutionary designs and had embarked on a
desperate endeavour. This was less true of his disciples. It is
easy to understand how these popular confusions arose.

His disciples bared their teeth at the English and at Edinburgh respectability in the Rose Street pubs. Drunkennness was
esteemed; sex was optional, and more honoured in the ode than
the observance. During the war and later, the Café Royal was
the scene of their foregatherings after dark, as the London
Café Royal had housed the English bohemia of the Twenties.
There it was that Hector allegedly sent back his dubious lobsters, and there it was, so the story went, that he knocked down
Gilbert Harding, the BBC's itinerant pundit, for calling him 'a
bloody Highlander'. Not all the contemptuous behaviour of
MacDiarmid's men rang true, and they sometimes seemed
boastful and sorry for themselves. George Barker's recent satire
on an evening spent drinking at the Abbotsford would have
been just as near the knuckle had it been written ten years
before:

> And on each shoulder
> Like a rowan
> A chip that goes on
> Growing, growing . . .

Several of them shrank from Jamieson's *Dictionary*, as consulted
by MacDiarmid, and settled instead for a dialect verse shorn
of its original country context and wrenched to accommodate
the imaginings of Colinton and Corstorphine.

This is not to deny that the Lallans movement could appear
to offer stirring prospects. I remember the eagerness with which
I used to follow an anthology of Lallans poems run by J. M.
Reid, the editor of the *Bulletin*: it included Douglas Young's
translation from the Gaelic of George Campbell Hay, 'Thonder
they ligg on the grund o the sea.' Glimpsed like this in translation, the Gaelic poetry of Sorley MacLean was held in great
respect. Certain novelists, too, were admired as confederates:
Neil Gunn, Fionn MacColla and Eric Linklater. The view from
Regent Road in the early hours, towards the planes and de-
clivities of the sleeping Lothians, took in a landscape that was
far from benighted, a hinterland where contributing poets and
pamphleteers lay in their suburbs and country cottages. Hector's
friend, Sydney Goodsir Smith, wrote a Lallans which was the
opposite of esoteric and which served very well for the verse
narratives, the bohemian episodes and extravaganzas, which he
went in for at this stage (the 'Saltire Modern Poets' series said
of him in 1947: 'his spirit is high though his flesh is deplorably
weak'). But I now think that the most accomplished of the
writers in Scots, apart from MacDiarmid, was Robert Garioch.
His diction consulted no dictionaries and was a natural, guttural
Scots: it never suggested that he had *resolved* to write that way.
Scots is a language you can be funny in, but you'd never think
it when you read Lallans—except for MacDiarmid and Garioch's.
'Queer Ongauns' has him sighting a civic motorcade:

> a beadle of some sort displayin
> frae ilk front sait a muckle gowden cosh:
> shame on them aa, whatever they were daein!

I first saw Hugh MacDiarmid and the poet Norman MacCaig
on the same day. The occasion was a meeting of the Saltire
Society in their rooms at Gladstone's Land in the High Street.
The meeting was addressed by MacDiarmid in an austere and
reproving manner which reminded me of other communist
sympathisers whom I knew in and around Edinburgh. I had a
relative who was a bit like that: just as MacDiarmid had combined communism with an enthusiasm for Social Credit, so she
had felt tender towards both Hitler and Stalin. In both cases, I
guessed, what soldered these loyalties together, so to speak,
was this minatory bearing, this air of punishing rectitude,

109

Passionaria-like as opposed to the mere *appassionata* of the other Lallans Makars, Himmler-like by comparison with the Heines you found in the Abbotsford. As it turned out, I was wrong—in MacDiarmid's case. The people's poet is also extremely conversable. But on that evening he was all severity: the element of a just threat was completed by some audience-scolding references to Polish literary theorists, delivered in what sounded like a kind of cut-glass working-class accent. I had never before listened to anyone talking about weighty subjects in a voice like that. Out of an attaché-case lolled long tongues of typescript covered in quotations from Baltic scholars.

After the meeting I was introduced by Hector to a MacCaig made pensive, perhaps, by those Baltic scholars and that platform manner. One night shortly afterwards I ran into him again in the vestibule of the General Post Office, where we spent an hour talking about the imagery of Lorca. The GPO was the hub of the Edinburgh I have been describing, with its wild lives, its prim lives, the 'heavenly Hanoverianism'—in Burns's phrase—of its handsome squares and thoroughfares, and the loyal names that were prudently conferred on these by the magistrates who built the New Town: facing me across a street sloe-black in the rain was the Café Royal, to my right was Regent Road, Regent Terrace and the Royal High School, to my left was Princes Street, and at my back was the Royal Mile. MacCaig did not seem to mind spending an hour talking about Lorca with a schoolboy he hardly knew (only Lorca, we said, could have provided that image of a bisected apple), and the encounter was typical of the town as I knew it then, of its grave interest in literature and of its private courtesy.

In those days MacCaig was still a Surrealist or Apocalyptic poet—at times, and in the manner of the times, very obscure. What is rather unusual, his best vein or veins have come with middle age. 'Landscape,' he told me 20 years later, 'is my religion.' He has written a poetry of faithful natural description: Edinburgh's trams, now gone, used to

> Lower themselves like bugs on a branch down
> The elbow of the Mound.

Yet there is religion there too, and the religion to which he is moved by landscape, and by love, has a theological tendency which faintly recalls the fine points and split hairs of bygone Scotch Platonists and Hegelians, and which can almost be judged to be ethnic or indigenous (though these are words you do well to avoid in Scotland, and words which he himself would not wish his critics to use). He is a metaphysical poet as well as a landscape poet, though I like him better myself in the second role; a poet of conceits as well as of descriptions, of parts and wholes as well as of bugs on a branch. What is possibly a little exotic is his feeling for the lyric as a craft which is also a game and a pleasure. This, I think, has supplied a good deal of his staying-power.

It is only in the last few years that he has had anything like due honour in Scotland. His sort of lyric is of course a lonely business, and is frequently denied early, or any, rewards. He may have been thought insufficiently Scottish, and he has been blamed for being insufficiently public and political. In fact, the climate of opinion, and MacDiarmid's authority, being what they were, his insistence on not writing in Scots, or in dudgeon, showed rare character. No portrait of Edinburgh would be accurate which evoked a community in which decent causes and sound talents were widely recognised as such, and MacCaig's fortunes not only as a poet but as a primary school teacher are a case in point. He has made his money, in Dylan Thomas's words, as a teacher, and he has applied more than once for a headmastership, to be turned down on the grounds—insofar as any grounds could be deduced or surmised—that he was a conscientious objector in the First World War. His distinction as a poet had not, it seems, reached the Education Committee, or was held against him; and to this day he remains an assistant primary school headmaster, a canny category, though he has been asked to lecture by the University. The solemn imported art occasions, commercial junketings and civic motorcades of the Edinburgh Festival have caused the citizens to be even more indifferent than before to their own writers, and most of these felt estranged from the public life of the place. From the city fathers they expected nothing.

Unlike those of MacCaig, Hector MacIver's talents—other than his teaching talents, that's to say—were exercised in a craft for which institutional facilities, and indeed civic support, are commonly required. In 1958 he married Mary Brown, also a teacher, and moved to Temple, continuing for the rest of his life to teach at the Royal High, and continuing to produce plays at the school, some of which were written by his pupils. I am sure he would have done well as a director in the theatre, but then there was very little theatre for him to do well in. Equally, he was an outstanding broadcaster both in Gaelic and in English, but as time went on he was heard less and less frequently on the Scottish BBC, which had a dismal record during these years in the matter of putting interesting and thoughtful people on the air. Hector did not regard teaching as a second best: he taught as his ancestors fought—with a whole heart. And there were other courses open to him which he did not choose to take. But the point is that he did not want to live in London, and that the story of his life is in part the story of what happens when too many of the materials for a vigorous and progressive cultural life have been transferred to the metropolis. Not all institutions and openings have gone south. But I can't easily imagine, for instance, that a good feature film with Scottish characters will ever be made.

Scotland made him suffer in other ways too. In *Scottish Country*, the collection of essays edited by George Scott-Moncrieff and published in 1935, Hector described the mean and brutal role played by the Presbyterian Church in the Hebrides.

As interpreted by the Presbyterian ministers of the Hebrides, life is identified with asceticism and repression. The crucifixion of the body is the monotonous theme of all their discourses. Drinking, dancing, music and recreation are officially condemned. But these gentlemen in their fanatical and destructive campaign forget that such taboos cannot be imposed on country people, whose nature it is to set more store on human values than on ascetic ones. And the more their human wants are denied them, the more they tend to excess. So that in the Isles the arts of drinking and dancing are still in a very healthy condition, for when they have to be pursued in secret, they become an exciting adventure. To this extent the people have managed to resist the self-mortifying demands of the Church —and the fact that fresh songs are brought forth yearly from the Western Isles would seem to indicate that there is no deterioration in the art of music. But these are not new songs; they are traditional things that have managed to survive in spite of difficulties. The creative impulse in the arts has been successfully stifled by the Church—except in the Catholic islands where the gospel of humanism receives more of its due. If anybody were now to produce a chant of such pagan and sensual beauty as the Dawn Prayer of Clan Ranald, which Dr Alexander Carmichael found in the Hebrides, he would probably be brought to account by the Church. Yet the hymns and incantations of *Carmina Gadelica* reveal a philosophy of much greater beauty and spiritual depth than anything now known within the Protestant Church of the Isles.

'The arts of drinking and dancing' . . . What about the art of love? Hector used to tell a story about lords and ladies on the deck of some Highland boat—in their dainty, cork-heeled shoon, you might say. It began to rain, and for the ladies' sake they called down into the hold: 'Was there a mackintosh?' 'No,' came the answer. 'But there is a Macleod who is well spoken of.' What, then, about the Macleods who were well spoken of?

Their absence from Hector's description is interesting, for there can be no doubt that the exciting adventures of love persisted in the Western Isles along with the drinking and dancing, and in the same clandestine fashion. Nevertheless, despite their absence, the passage has an excellent forthrightness about it: it reads as if delivered on oath. To make such a case against the Church might appear to have been old-fashioned or anachronistic, but in 1935 the power of the Church was by no means spent, and I can't believe it is spent even now. How far, indeed, did the power of the Church survive in his own nature? The influence of a strong-willed mother may have made religion something that was easier to forswear than to escape from, and it is unlikely that he ever really escaped.

Pursued in secret, the arts of drinking and dancing 'became an exciting adventure'. The existence in his youth of this Hebridean underground may help to explain why you occasionally felt that the grown, expatriate MacIver remained a man of secrets (though he was never a dancer). Secrecy was more a matter of style with him than of items to be, or not to be, divulged, and as such it may help to explain why he can be

H                                              113

considered a romantic. Romanticism is associated historically with the challenge to the Church's authority which developed during the 19th century. The pursuit of the clandestine and the forbidden, and of excess, is romantic. Obscurity itself is romantic, and the criticised obscurity of Dylan Thomas and of the verse in *Schola Regia* may have appealed to his crepuscular side, so that the black art of modern poetry was not the least of his secrets.

I remember Hector relating how a young man had once, in a fit of shame, dived into Stornoway harbour in order to cleanse himself. Many Scotsmen have dived, or wired, into a bottle of whisky for the same reasons, and there is something provenly Scottish about Robert Graves's

Siamese twins: one, maddened by
The other's moral bigotry,
Resolved at length to misbehave
And drink them both into the grave.

The tendency, of course, is for these twins to be lodged inside the one man. 'Asceticism and repression' are no joke but a painful and stubborn reality, which counts for more than the lack of cultural institutions has done, and which breeds 'the violent dreamed escape'—in the words of another poet, Thom Gunn—through drink or through a strenuous, murderous sexuality, a wiring into women. It has also bred this tradition of conviviality and talk: the passion in the Rose Street pubs has to be heard to be believed. One way or another, many Scotsmen have made their bed in the bar, that fine and private place of public resort, and suffered out their secrets there.

In writing about the Edinburgh of 20 years ago I have tried not to let my memories of the time be overruled by hindsight, and it is possible that some of the emotion I felt in the middle of the night in Regent Road was, as it were, glandular, a consequence of growing up. There may have been less going on than I thought. After all, the Modern Movement was ancient history by then: the 'Scottish Renaissance' was inaugurated in the Twenties, and a number of the old hands had given it up for dead after the war; Lallans was no novelty, and the men of sorrow had been feuding with MacDiarmid whole decades before.

What happened after the war, I now consider, was that a

literary tradition chiefly derived from 19th-century Romanticism was exposed to the claims of a freshly assertive nationalism and Modernism. These two forces—both significantly, of foreign origin—had come late to Scotland: there is evidence of mounting energies during the Thirties, certainly on the Nationalist front, but the war imposed a moratorium. After the war there was hope of a leap forward.

Fidelity to the romantic canon did not prevent you from leaping—romanticism itself was full of leaps. A subsequent fidelity to Eliot's classicism was not held to involve any impossible contradiction, as I have said, and this is a matter which deserves to be looked at further. The emphasis placed by Scottish Nationalists on the native product was permitted to veil the fact that both nationalism and Modernism were imports. Nationalism was originally associated with various European upheavals and with romantic literary modes, but a change occurred early in this century, as a result of which it became linked with classicism instead. The change began in France, and its main advocate would appear to have been the fascist, Charles Maurras, whose writ was to run extensively through the literary criticism of Western Europe even after the activities of the Nazis had made him a black author. A recent writer, Mr H. R. Kedward, has studied his precepts, and has this to say: according to Maurras, 'the national critic, looking for a criterion of beauty, will find it by observing the accepted and persistent cultural tradition of his country. For France, this was obviously the classical tradition.' Under the influence of Maurras among others, Eliot's criterion became classical too, though not even the most sympathetic can have found it altogether easy to relate to an observation of the accepted and persistent cultural traditions of England and America. The attempt to relate a classical standard to the cultural tradition of Scotland must have seemed more formidable still, and the 'national critics' who spoke up there in succeeding years were mostly inclined to concentrate on the patriotic element in such prescriptions as that of Maurras and to accord a separate and secondary homage to the classical, working hard at the not exactly straightforward tack of reconciling it with the Modern. Meanwhile romantic values reigned on regardless.

As interpreted by French Catholic writers like Maurras,

115

nationalism entailed not only classicism but right-wing politics and anti-semitism. Romantics were apt to be placed in the same category as socialists and Jews. This sort of thing was never likely to do very well in Scotland, but in Europe generally it has to be seen as one of the more influential varieties of Modernism. Modernism took a quite different form, of course, in the case of MacDiarmid, who chose to be a Modernist, a nationalist, a communist and a romantic. And other combinations and permutations were also tried in Scotland. A welter of thoughts survived from the Thirties into the post-war period— thoughts which the experience of the war had done little to amend or define, and which were current partly in the form of arbitrary and contradictory injunctions, of advanced or reactionary notions separated from the pain of their original occasions. Heterogeneous ideas were yoked together by violence and by innocence, the right hand did not always know what its left hand was doing, and MacDiarmid's signs flashed left and right alternately. In such a situation no one could feel much confidence in applying terms like 'romantic' or 'communist' to any of the writers concerned.

In the *Memorials of his Time* Henry Cockburn (another alumnus of the High School) told of 'the change from ancient to modern manners' which came about in Edinburgh at the end of the 18th century; and he did so in a clear and solid classical prose which nonetheless responded to the advent of Romanticism, to the ethos that accompanied the gathering fame of Walter Scott, for whom Edinburgh had become 'mine own romantic town'. Now, after 150 years of the romantic, it is possible to chronicle a further change from ancient to modern manners. The field, however, is far narrower: modern manners entered the literature of the time but other walks of Edinburgh life went untouched. And this in itself is a pointer to one of the differences between Cockburn's Edinburgh and Hector MacIver's. Cockburn's single town had become several, had been drowned in a fair-sized city; the professions no longer had much to do with one another, nor did the social classes. Someone, though, who did move in more than one world was Hector's friend and physician, Chalmers Davidson. Cockburn would have approved of a distinguished medical man who knows about books, and admired his appearance: that domed, judicious

116

head would have looked well at bowls or claret with the old *cognoscenti*. And despite all that had been lost, modern Edinburgh had other worthies, many a milieu, and many an anecdote, that would have pleased Cockburn's sort of connoisseur. The old habits of courtesy, conviviality and the discussion of literature were still observed. As in Cockburn's day, the conversing *cognoscenti* still tramped the Pentland Hills.

Modern manners are usually felt to be, in some sense, 'free'. If Eliot is correct in insisting that the facts of innovation in literature are hard work, a recourse to the past and the search for a superior precision, the sentiments of innovation, for all that, are sentiments of freedom. 'Freedom' was the word in post-war Edinburgh—in art as in love: that touching expression, 'free love', was still available to the adolescent, and it seemed to belong to the general Caledonian Thaw that was in the air. The end of a war is a good time for thaws, no doubt, and there were others in the world then. When I first went south I noticed among Sassenach choreographers that classical ballet was known to be doomed (despite the supposed prevalence of classical standards in the other arts), that it was a form of slavery, that dance was about to lose its chains and become Free Dance. Free Dance, Free Verse, Free Love, Free Milk—thus, restoring the watchwords of the Twenties, we leapt and leapt.

Like all freedoms, this one—to the extent that it existed outside the minds of the young and was ever practised—fell through. It is worth comparing it with the experience of the leaping students of the present time. *Their* revolution has largely to be reckoned a practical and political affair, by virtue of their interest in the problems of democracy, of 'participation', that arise in industrial societies. This one was not a revolution at all but more a state of mind, a private matter which made hardly any stir, with the stress on art rather than politics. Both 'revolutions', however, have been intent on liberating people's sexual lives, so that young men would no longer feel the need to dive into harbours and wire into religion or whisky: I respect this aim myself, and salute it. At the time, Scottish Nationalism seemed to me, in a political sense, rather peripheral: it seemed like a kind of anti-politics—at once a vengeance on Westminster and an escape from the conventional subject-matter of the politics of industrial societies, and from their insoluble economics. And

I am not sure it has changed much in the intervening 20 years. Scotland, perhaps, is the land of escapes—of actual or imagined flights and emigrations.

Even at the time, I was sceptical about Lallans and about literary nationalism, though they seemed an agreeable constituent of the new freedom, and authentically modern. I thought then—and I still think this is fundamental—that literature was indivisible and should not be parcelled according to political, patriotic or linguistic prescriptions. Lorca mattered more to me and my friends than Compton Mackenzie did. Boys read English books and were conditioned ('over-conditioned,' says Hugh MacDiarmid) to write in English, and if Conrad was allowed to do it, why shouldn't we be? Brought up in Edinburgh, Muriel Spark has written in English about Scottish life, and *The Prime of Miss Jean Brodie* is a valuable picture of the Edinburgh of the Thirties. (Miss Brodie, who felt tender towards Mussolini, might just conceivably have read some Maurras in the original, which could not be said of the rest of the *literati*. She is the embodiment of a certain kind of Scottish teacher, the Preceptor and Muse, and her school is not all that unlike the Royal High in Hector's day. It may even be that a few of the essays in the present collection are not all that unlike the tribute which Miss Brodie's pupils, her famous 'set', might have wished to pay her.) But although Muriel Spark is on any serious estimate the foremost living Scottish novelist, she has yet to be admitted to the Northern pantheon. In the same way, the Anglophile Drummond of Hawthornden is 'only nominally represented' in *The Oxford Book of Scottish Verse*.

Hector MacIver recognised the stupidity of enforcing such categories, and he did not blame writers for leaving Scotland or for not writing in Scots or about 'Scottish' subjects: the patriotism which ignored or disparaged them was rejected entirely. The Scotland he cared about included its diaspora. I think he would have accepted that Lord Reith is as much a phenomenon of Scottish culture as Hugh MacDiarmid, whom in some respects he resembles; that John Buchan, whose romanticism led him to Oxfordshire, Westminster and Canada, is as Scottish as Compton Mackenzie, whose romanticism led him to settle in the Hebrides and finally in Edinburgh's New Town; that no account of 19th-century Scottish cultural history can afford to neglect such expatriates as Carlyle, or even such expatriate stock as the Mills.

Recently Scottish Nationalism has taken another leap and has scored impressive electoral successes. Even so, I can't myself regard secession as either probable or desirable. Unless I am far wrong about the lives described in this memoir, they do not contribute to the case for a total severance, though they certainly do suggest that Scotland should have more of its own in the way of institutions and opportunities. The state of Scotland represents a considerable part of the case for the regionalised Britain which is now being talked about.

There is evidence enough in the world for distrusting federal solutions; and there have been recent secessions of overwhelming merit, whose failure has to be seen as a disaster not only for the countries in question but for all countries. Nationalism, however, has been grossly over-praised, and the emotions with which the subject of political autonomy has been invested are a poor guide to its capacity to serve the best interests of the societies that show signs of aspiring to it. The French Canadian Prime Minister of Canada, Pierre Trudeau, published a diatribe a few years ago against the idea of an independent Quebec, in which he imagines what the coming generation of French Canadians may feel about it. 'What! they will say to the intellectuals, you did so little writing and so little thinking and yet you had time to ruminate over separatism?' Violent as they are, the following words of his can be commended to the attention of Scotsmen, who will not need to be advised to make allowance for the different circumstances of Scottish life:

> The ultimate tragedy would be in not realising that French Canada is too culturally anaemic, too economically destitute, too intellectually retarded, too spiritually paralysed, to be able to survive more than a couple of decades of stagnation, emptying herself of all her vitality into nothing but a cesspit, the mirror of her nationalistic vanity and 'dignity'.

The example of French Canada is one to depress Scottish Nationalists—if only because the election of a French Canadian premier will not assist the arrival of a *Quebec libre*. And the example of Ireland can no longer be as encouraging to Scottish Nationalists as it was at first. Should they struggle tooth and nail to achieve something like the present state of that country, which is hardly prosperous, and in which the power of the Church and of parish politicians, and of narrow-minded respectability, has been consolidated? In Scotland that same power exists, and it could not fail to grow larger in secession. Scottish Nationalism, at any rate, has never shown that there is any other sort of sovereignty in prospect.

# 8

## Old Songs and New Poetry

### by Sorley MacLean

A few months ago my brother John, who is as well qualified to give an opinion as anyone I know, said that the greatest of all Scottish works of art is *Cumha na Cloinne*, the 'Lament for the Children', attributed by the tradition of pipers to Patrick Mór MacCrimmon and therefore of the 17th century. I hardly demurred, but suggested that, if it is not *Cumha na Cloinne* or some other one of the great pibrochs, it is one of those Gaelic songs of the two and a half centuries between 1550 and 1800—the songs in which ineffable melodies rise like exhalations from the rhythms and resonances of the words, the songs that alone make the thought that the Gaelic language is going to die so intolerable to anyone who knows Gaelic and has in the least degree the sensibility that responds to the marriage, or rather the simultaneous creation, of words and music. It may be that a great piper without Gaelic can play a great pibroch supremely; it may even be that a great singer without much Gaelic can be coached into a great singing of one of those songs; but it is certain that no one who does not know Gaelic can really hear one of those songs. Perhaps one or another of the great pibrochs is in itself a greater thing than any single one of the songs, but there are so many more great songs than great pibrochs that I am convinced that Scottish Gaelic song is the chief artistic glory of the Scots, and of all peoples of Celtic speech, and one of the greatest artistic glories of Europe. I have been of this opinion for nearly 40 years, I have reiterated it *ad nauseam*, and now I am more convinced of its validity than I have ever been. I am no musician, and I can well imagine one of our fine pipers making about me the kind of remark that Gogarty made to Francis George Scott about Yeats, after listening to Scott and

121

Yeats arguing about words and music. Like many others, I believe that there has never been a great song that is not a great poem too, and I believe with Croce that all poetry is 'lyrical', that verse now and again, but rarely, arrives at a point at which it utters the 'lyrical cry'.

There are now in the archives of the School of Scottish Studies something like 6,000 separate Gaelic melodies, and it can be taken for granted that many of them can be called 'great'. A song like the Campbell/Morrison *Ailean Donn*, or the Mac-Lean *Ailean Donn, Cairistìona*, or the 'Jura Islands', or *Mac Sìri*, or *Iain Garbh*, or 'Young Margaret', or any of two or three MacGregor songs, is an art beyond art when it is well sung, and it is still great poetry to one who has never heard it sung. I am, for instance, quite sure that I thought 'On the level of the road' one of the greatest of all Scottish poems long before I knew that there was extant a melody for it, which I heard for the first time from the late Mrs Buchanan Dunlop (Cathy Clark) in 1948.

If the words only of those old songs were extant, if the melodies were all lost, the songs could not fail to be a perennial stimulus to Gaelic poets. But since both melodies and words are extant for very many of them, the stimulus to some poets is so great as to be almost destructive. In the Thirties of this century something happened to articulate Gaels (by 'articulate' I mean likely to express their views more or less publicly) which had not happened for 100 years before. It was as if a French child of some peasant family near Chartres or Rheims, after being inside these cathedrals, had been taken away to some English industrial town where the only Gothic architecture was a few Victorian churches; as if he had lived there and had never seen a picture of a French or English medieval church until, in his late teens, he went back to the French cathedrals. In 1930 the 'image' of Gaelic song was to almost all articulate Gaels only as mediocre Victorian Gothic is to the Gothic of the 12th or 13th centuries. By 1930 there was beginning to be a difference, and as the Thirties went on, more and more Gaels were boldly proclaiming where the real artistic glories of their people lay. Among those Gaels Hector MacIver was one of the keenest sensibilities, and his eloquence was such that while he was still an undergraduate, or soon after, he was being mentioned with

Maxton as one of the foremost Scottish orators of the day. He was also one of the few Gaels whose moral courage equalled his physical courage, and he had as much physical courage as any man I have known.

The Celtic Twilight of the 1890s and its product, the *Songs of the Hebrides*, were to the realities of Gaelic song poetry as Victorian Gothic is to the North French cathedrals. There is, however, in Gaelic song such an intrinsic quality of poetry and music that some of it could not fail to come through again and again, even in the *Songs of the Hebrides*, just as there is such a quality in Gothic architecture that it often shines through sham Gothic. In the 1920s, therefore, much 'educated' Gaelic opinion was right in preferring the *Songs of the Hebrides* to almost all 19th-century Gaelic song, which now seems, to me at any rate, to have been a natural product of the Clearances, the Evangelical Revival and the Education Act of 1872.

The Clearances removed most of the Gaelic-speaking people to the industrial Lowlands and to Canada and Australia, vastly aggravated the poverty of those left crowded on the poorest patches of land in the Highlands and Islands, and broke their spirit. The Evangelical Revival proved with Fundamentalist and Calvinist logic that this world is only 'a vale of tears' and that the faithful must bear all the iniquities heaped on them by the powers that be, which are ordained by God, and that this world's material acquisitions do not matter at all. When the effects of the Evangelical Revival were abating, the Education Act began to teach children to sing 'Hearts of Oak' instead of *Cairistìona, Cabar-féidh* or *Beinn Dòrain*. The 'spiritual' leaders who were not Free Church Evangelicals went to Balmoral, and for the sake of the Anglo-Scottish Establishment, of which they were a part, preached nauseous propaganda against their fellow Gaels of Ireland. Even if the Free Church ministers could have brought Victoria and all the Establishment to some Gaelic Canossa, they would not have thought it worthwhile, knowing that she and almost all of her Establishment would soon have to endure fires worse than the Canossa snows.

In the terrible late 18th century and the worse 19th century, the years from 1780 to 1870, when Anglicised land-capitalist Highland chiefs with Gaelic names all but destroyed their blood kindred in order to fill their own pockets, Gaelic song poetry

123

degenerated to a feeble wail and to a feebler pietism; what was healthy became parochial. In those years most of the real spiritual quality of the Gaelic-speaking people was expressed in the almost wholly extempore and unrecorded sermons and prayers of ministers and 'men' to whom all poetry and song except the Psalms of David was one of the more seductive vanities of this vale of tears. If only a moderate fraction of those sermons and prayers had been recorded, however, Scottish Gaelic would have a great 19th-century prose. Even as late as the 1920s it was quite common to hear some minister or elder quoting richly, by oral tradition, from sermons or prayers delivered 70 or 100 years before. Such quotations made it quite plain that in frankness, sincerity and psychological insight, expressed with an astonishing wealth of imagery and illustration, sometimes sonorously eloquent with the incomparable resonances of the Gaelic language and sometimes racily colloquial, Gaelic once had a great prose. If a man of imagination is convinced of the rags of human righteousness and of the desperate wickedness of the human heart, the expression of his conviction cannot fail to be powerful. Even to this day there may be heard Gaelic sermons in which the thought is essentially that of St Augustine, Calvin or even Pascal, and the prose one of great tension and variety. I fully believe that I have never heard or read as great a Gaelic prose as I have heard in the unrecorded sermons of Ewen MacQueen.

I also believe that this almost lost prose had far more impact on modern Gaelic poets than the prose, for instance, of Norman MacLeod, who was regarded until recently as the 'greatest' Gaelic prose-writer. I am sure that, compared with the lost prose of John MacDonald of Ferintosh, that of Norman Mac-Leod is merely orotund pietistic parochialism crossed with the parochialism of Balmoral. The Balmoral variety confirmed the parochialism that was imposed on Gaelic literature by the impotence of the 19th-century Scottish Gael in the face of the Clearances, and aggravated that post-1746 sense of inferiority which induced so many educated Gaels to derive an undue amount of comfort from the impact on Europe of James (Ossian) Macpherson. A few months ago, hearing the doyen of international Celtic scholars exalt James Macpherson largely because of his impact on Europe, I felt impelled to commend to his attention a much greater Macpherson (Mary), of whom he had apparently never heard. One trouble is, or was, that men of industry and critical intellect comparable to the many who had worked on Celtic philology, and Scottish Gaelic philology in particular, had never applied themselves to Gaelic poetry, or at any rate to the Gaelic poetry of Scotland. I vividly remember my own thrill in 1933 when Mr James Caird and Dr George Davie introduced me to *Sangschaw* and *A Drunk Man Looks at the Thistle*, and I found, *inter alia plurima*, that Hugh MacDiarmid had sensed the greatness of Alexander MacDonald. Looking back now, I realise that the native sense of inferiority was part of my gratification at finding some genuine if one-sided appreciation of 18th-century Gaelic poetry in the man, a Lowland Scot, who I then felt, and still feel, had written some of the greatest European poetry of the century. I do not presume to be a judge of comparative European poetry, but the Nobel Laureates, Yeats and Eliot, are both, I think, inferior to MacDiarmid. If I remember rightly, I did not in 1933, nor do I now, put Alexander MacDonald's poetry on the same high level as the obscure or anonymous songs of 1550 to 1800, but it is very difficult to think of those songs as poetry alone. Their impact can never be that of poetry alone, though as such they are great enough for me. Their duality does, however, make them a dilemma to the modern Gaelic poet, whom they may fill with despair.

By the second half of the 18th century Gaelic poetry had known some wonderful triumphs in the realisation of physical nature. In a kind of objectivity it had gone as far as poetry can go, certainly further than any poetry I know in English, French or Latin. But it is deficient in explicit humanity. Duncan Macintyre can realise the great sweep of a mountain or the different motions of stags and hinds on it, or the eddying of a spring on its shoulder; MacDonald can realise the thump and plash of a ship's fore-quarters, or the sob under its aft-quarters, or the squirting race of a rope over its gunwale or through a cleat. Both can do such things as no one else, I believe, has ever done them in any language I know. But the physical scene is in itself far more important than either the explicit human reaction to it or its place as a background to human activity. Its appeal is overmuch to the senses rather than the heart or the brain, and though I do not discount its implicit emotion of joy, I think that it lacks the power to move most people deeply. In essence, its effect is something like a transcendent triumph of the Imagist programme of English and American poets in the first 20 years of this century.

In this same second half of the 18th century, however, the saintly Dugald Buchanan was expressing with a terrible clarity and intensity the Pauline-Augustinian-Calvinist reaction to the dispensation of the universe. His poetry is at the very opposite pole from that of MacDonald and Macintyre. It is an explicit expression of human love pitted in acceptance against a pre-conceived theistic view of the universe; it is the inevitable resolution of Calvinist passion. His poetry is at the opposite pole, too, from the inhuman sexual passion of this 16th-century song, though the modern reader may see a likeness:

> You burned my stackyard of oats and barley,
> You killed my father and my husband,
> Yes, and my three young brothers;
> Though you did that, I rejoice that you are alive.
> I like dark Allan from Lundy,
> My love the brown-haired coated Allan.
> I like dark Allan from Lundy.

It is a sad and ironic comment on the inadequacy of contemporary evaluations of poetry that in the Eighties and Nineties of the last century Scotland had in Mary Macpherson a major Gaelic poet when Edinburgh, Dublin, London and Paris thought that the vapid Celtic Twilight was the only poetic habitat of the Gael. She, too, is the antithesis of Dugald Buchanan. Nineteenth-century Gaelic poetry is at its best in her when she mingles in it her sorrows and humiliation, the destruction of her people by the Clearances, her great *joie de vivre* and her perplexity that the remnant of her people have grown so 'strange' that 'sorrow is wheat to them', her holding fast to her own worldly pride and 'vanity', the plant that 'satisfies the flesh'. She is one of the few 19th-century Scottish Gaels of stature who did not dismiss the world in exchange for the ecstasies of the Evangelical Revival, or who were not so broken by the breaking of their people that their poetic voices became mouthpieces for parochialism and moralising. In her, echoes of the old songs

126

are heard far oftener and more authentically than in any other
19th-century Gaelic poet. Indeed the old songs, gone underground except in the Catholic islands, were often more or less
secretly in the mouths of people who refused to accept the
orthodoxy that no worth while 'criticism of life' in glorious
words, that was not ostensibly religious, had ever come from
Gaelic lips. In Raasay about 40 years ago, an old woman of
impeccable Free Church antecedents once said of the Psalmist:
'David, the dirty blackguard, what was he compared with William Ross!' I myself consider William Ross's last song one of
the very greatest poems ever made in any language in the
islands once called British, but I do not think of it nearly as
often as I do of some of the old songs. I think of it, however,
more often than I do of any poem by MacDonald or Macintyre.

I suppose the poet is the musician *manqué*, but just as surely
the musician is the poet *manqué*, because 'this intellectual being,
the thoughts that wander through eternity', are at most only
implicit in the musician's art. As poetry, the old Gaelic song has
everything except our modern world and the far-ranging, un-
inhibited, troubled, explicit modern intellect; and because it has
what it has, and is the supreme aesthetic product of our Gaelic-
speaking people, it is bound to be one of the major influences
on even the most modern Gaelic poet who is not altogether
*déraciné* and ready to swallow unmixed the latest poetic theory
from London, New York, Paris or Moscow. I think that all
modern Gaelic poets, even those out at forward observation
posts on the European poetical battlefield, would agree with me
in this. On the European front itself, it is this necessity for an
intellectually satisfying content that remains art which has produced Symbolism, and Symbolism, in its manifestations in Blok,
Yeats, Valéry, Rilke, MacDiarmid and Eliot, is the most impressive 'ism' that I know of in this century.

Gaelic song before 1800 has everything except complexity of
explicit thought, and it affords a variety of the many kinds of
utterance that Arnold calls 'criticism of life'. Think of Fraser of
Reelig's daughter regretting the three things that come un-
asked; or John MacLean holding off his passion for the Campbell woman, with his unbending tree and ebb followed by flood;
or the unknown poet accepting his loss of East, West, North
and South, and his loss 'almost' of God. It has supreme passion

held at the shortest arm's length compatible with art or the longest arm's length consistent with passion. It has the consolation of the woman raped at the shieling and forsaken, that she still has kinsmen and probably a lover among the splendid MacDonalds with the glories of Auldearn on their arms; the bitter grief and mixed love of the Campbell wife of MacLean of Coll hearing of the slaughter of her brave kinsmen at Inverlochy by the 'bad' clans, with her husband and son among them, the MacDonalds and the MacLeans; the magical evocations of external nature in such songs as those attributed to Donald of Bohuntin and 'The Braes of Locheil', the 'Heir of Strath Swordale's Daughter', *Mac Sìri*, the song of the Kintail outlaw Farquhar MacRae in his cave in Coire Gorm a' Ghlinne behind Ben Attow, of John MacRae on the run from the Yankees about 1780, remembering his going up and down through Glen Shiel and Torr-Laoisich of the song-thrushes.

In the impressive 'Notes on the Border Ballads' in his book *Latitudes*, Edwin Muir had some significant and even moving things to say about those great Lowland poems. He talks of them as contemplating life in the light of pure passion. More often than not, the Gaelic song does not have this pure passion. It offers a breathtaking evocation of the natural background as well as passion as great as words can hold, and since human life and the human heart are subtle and 'impure', I believe that, partly because of this, the greatest Gaelic songs are greater poems than the greatest of the Lowland Ballads. For those who know Gaelic I need mention only the 'heavy surge and the deep kyle' in *Cairistìona*, or the 'little birch hollow' in 'Come, my love', or the glimpse of moonrise in the song of the woman who has lost her five children, 'Girl over yonder'. There are many examples of such a counterpointing of suffering and of a kind of Yeatsian 'joy'.

Celtic poetry has frequently, and rightly, been accused of rhetoric, of excessive stylisation, of a too elaborate and self-conscious technique. Far too much of the technical virtuosity of the Bardic Schools overflowed into the vernacular Chief-and-Clan poetry of the 16th, 17th and 18th centuries. But it is not so with the old songs. There the poet is talking to himself—herself, more often—walking the tightrope of metre without being conscious of it: and it is never tighter than, until this century, was considered by European practice necessary to poetry. I am not going to enter the question of metre and Free Verse except to say that however tight the rope of auditory shape may be, there has nevertheless to be some kind of tightrope onto which the poet goes. I am not prepared to allow to the word 'rhythm' the vagueness sanctioned by much contemporary theory in Britain, Europe and America. Metre does not make poetry, but I am not satisfied that poetry can exist without it. Perhaps it is as the 'filthy rags of human righteousness' are to the Calvinist Elect.

One seldom or never hears in the old songs of Gaeldom the rhythmic stumblings that one often hears in even the greatest of the Lowland Ballads. It can be argued that these flaws in the Ballads are due to generations of oral transmission, but why do they occur so seldom in Gaelic songs, which have undergone oral transmission for as many generations? In the Gaelic song the obvious corruption is often as breathtaking as the undoubted original—in total imaginative effect as well as in rhythm or metre. One undoubted quatrain on the execution, in 1570, of Gregor of Glenstrae reads as follows:

> I reached the meadow of Bealach,
> And there I got no peace;
> I did not leave a hair of my head unpulled
> Or skin on my hands.

That quatrain appears to have 'corrupted' to:

> I ascended the great mountain path with no stop for
>     breath,
> Before the day greyed [before morning twilight];
> I put the hair of my head to the ground
> And the skin of my two hands.

Metrically, the corruption is as good as the original.

Most of the new Gaelic poets are very much aware of the tremendous song poetry behind them, and I suspect that its effect on them is ambivalent. On the one hand, it is an emotional stimulus making for devotion to the marvellous Gaelic language. I frequently reread Sir Maurice Bowra's remarks on the Russian language in his introduction to *A Book of Russian Verse*, and I can never do so without applying to Gaelic much of what he says about the Russian language, and without being aware of a devotion to the Gaelic language among nearly all Gaelic poets, old and new, traditionalist and *avant-garde*, similar to the devotion to the Russian language which Bowra attributes to Turgenev. Nor can I read Bowra's words without being the more painfully aware of the intolerable situation of Scottish Gaelic today. For there is good reason to fear that the great song may soon be lost because there are no ears left to hear it. Modern Gaelic poetry may be, as an Appin man once put it 25 years ago, 'the last glimmer of the Gaelic sun before it goes down for ever'.

The Appin man's words referred in particular to what was new and vital in Gaelic poetry 25 years ago, but now, with what there is of 'new' as well as of more traditional Gaelic poetry, it looks as if there will be Gaelic Joshuas while there is a Gaelic language. We have the work of William Matheson, the Canna Campbells, the School of Scottish Studies, and of three now dead, my brother Calum, K. C. Craig and Hector MacIver, to keep all Gaels, and the new poets especially, alert to what is behind them. And we have the inspiring examples of the great tradition-bearers, of whom it is impossible not to mention Mr Calum Johnston. We owe more to him than to anyone else still alive.

Of those of whom I am thinking, Hector MacIver was almost unique, in that he was able to respond to the old and the new at the same time, and by virtue of his astonishing moral courage and his eloquence. He always maintained in conversation that what was in Gaelic would be Gaelic if it were worth while at all, no matter what foreign influences had gone to its genesis. That, I feel sure, is true. Certainly the Gael is a mixed, variable human being, and not a pasteboard creation looming in a twilight or anywhere else. Poetry must have some kind of universality in it, no matter what the local habitation and name. It is much the same, but different as well, with prose literature. With some unimportant changes, the central character of Mauriac's fine novel *La Pharisienne* could be a West Highland Seceder. The language itself, however, does in poetry constitute a difference so great as to be a difference in kind. I think I can apprehend the greatness of Mauriac fairly well without reading a word of him in French, but I cannot see greatness in Goethe, reading him in translation, and so I have to take it on trust that he is a great

130

poet. By the same token, neither I nor anyone else can ever hope to persuade the non-Gaelic world that William Ross's last song is comparable in quality to the best of Shakespeare's Sonnets. When Iain Crichton Smith talks of 'the infinite resonance' of William Ross, we know what he means, but the phrase is meaningless to anyone who does not know Gaelic.

The old songs may have a destructive influence on the modern Gaelic poet because of the danger that, no matter how many languages and literatures he knows well, the old Gaelic songs will remain for him the supreme hermaphrodite of words and music. It may be true on occasion, as with the 'Cro of Kintail' and the fragmentary words to one movement of *Cumha na Cloinne*, that the words are not anything to the music, but very often the simultaneous growth of both is such that after them one despairs of any human art of the ear. I know perfectly well that this is not fashionable talk nowadays, but to me no poetry, whatever it has of intellect or passion, or of delicacy and subtlety of perception, is great poetry unless it also has an auditory effect in proportion to one or more of its other qualities. Compared with that, 'purity' of diction is just one of the better products of sterility. The reduction to the absurd of the opposite view was achieved by editors who put in their anthologies MacDiarmid's 'Perfect' and rejected his 'Moonstruck'. (Morally, T. S. Eliot was one of them.) It is primarily this appeal to the ear which makes Yeats and the early MacDiarmid and, at a lower level, Eliot and Auden, such good poets. (I never shared Hector MacIver's reverence for Dylan Thomas.)

The old songs must be a burden on the new Gaelic poet if he has anything at all of Verlaine's feeling that poetry must be '*de la musique avant toute chose*'. I think that George Campbell Hay has felt the burden more lightly in that the music he seems to have most often at the back of his mind is the word music of the Bardic Schools, a more sophisticated, less intense, more attainable music that the 'out of this world' music of *Cairistìona*, 'Little Sister', 'Girl over yonder', 'The Jura Islands', *Mac Sìri*, 'I saw my lover', the two *Ailean Donn* songs and scores of others. To me George Campbell Hay's poetry has the virtuosity of genius and is an exquisite blend of the Bardic old and the new, but I think that Derick Thomson and I myself are always haunted by the more intense, piercing and lyrical

131

cry of the old songs. Because of that, we feel their burden more than Campbell Hay does. Of Crichton Smith, Donald Mac-Aulay and Donald MacLeod I am not sure. It may be that they do not feel the burden at all, but I hesitate to think that.

Sometimes I feel that people like myself ought to shut up about the old songs: talking about them may be trying to do something to young Gaelic poets that can bring to mind Yeats's pardonable illusion that words of his sent out 'certain men the English shot'. On the other hand, the ceaseless reiteration of the poetic qualities of Gaelic songs which some of us have carried on for about 30 years may at least be an antidote to the dead-pan flatness of contemporary English verse. England is big and near, and liable to be too much of an influence on the new Gaelic poet, especially if he is not the linguist that George Campbell Hay is. And, by the nature of things, the poet is seldom a good linguist.

To insist on the necessity for music in poetry may put one, I suppose, into the category that English literary criticism calls 'romantic', and it has been said again and again that the modern world and the atom bomb have eliminated romantic qualities from poetry. It seems to me that what 'romantic' means is largely a question of language, and I believe that all poetry may be called romantic in some way or other. The atom bomb, more than anything else, has brought about a change since 1945. But is this a change in kind rather than degree? The world was bad enough, and hopeless enough, between 1920 and 1930 when Scotland and the Anglo-Irish minority produced the great romantic poetry of Yeats and the early MacDiarmid, and certainly the *avant-garde* knew enough about Freud even then. It seems to me that to suggest that the atom bomb has destroyed romantic poetry for ever is equivalent to saying that it has destroyed all poetry except propaganda against the use of the bomb. This is to suggest that the final criterion of all poetry is a political or moral one, which is the same as saying that the final criterion of all human activity is political and moral, since men live in societies. It is also the same as saying that the final criterion is religious, if one believes in personal immortality. For Shelley the poet was the unacknowledged legislator of the world. For Dugald Buchanan he was, implicitly, the legislator for eternity, in which legislature the saintly Dugald Buchanan would have considered himself the obscurest of obscure backbenchers, but yet a member. The question is too big.

For the poet to believe, with the conscious mind at any rate, that the world may soon be turned to rubble by the atom bomb —is that radically different from believing, with the conscious mind, that 90 per cent of humanity, including nearly all those one loves most, are to spend an eternity of spiritual and physical torment? Poets have believed in an eternity of torment for the bulk of humanity and yet have continued to delight in love of all kinds and in external nature—in other words, have continued to be romantics. And I think they will continue to do so and be so even if they believe, with the conscious mind, that the world may soon be destroyed by atomic warfare. In the circumstances of our sub-atomic condition, it is romantic to put into pleasurable form the strange and complex, the mixed, greyish workings of the human heart. In spite of certain implications in Iain Crichton Smith's profound paper to the Gaelic Society of Inverness, poets and human beings will continue to be chancers; the preoccupation with the atomic bomb and with psychoanalytical honesty and linguistic 'purity' will have intervals of romantic voluptuousness. Perhaps these delights will be heightened by the prospect of the atomic holocaust, as those of William Ross must have been by the prospect of his own imminent death and his intellectual acceptance of Calvinism. It was only when he was actually dying that he asked for his poems to be burned.

The honesty that admits to the inhuman sexual passion of the woman who made the song for Allan of Lundy is fit to be an example of honesty in any poetry. If the insincerity of a great deal of Gaelic and English Victorian poetry is a long way from modern sincerity, it is an even longer way from the sincerity of the woman who loved Allan. With all his poses, snobberies and disgusting fascism, Yeats is to me a far more sincere poet than Eliot. Because of this sincerity, there shines through his poetry a deep, and romantic, envy of the noble plebeian James Connolly, not to mention Pearse, MacDonagh, and even his 'drunken vainglorious lout'. Even when Yeats is at his most rhetorical, one can sense the counterpointing of the sincere and the insincere, and I myself cannot see such a sincerity behind the preciously consistent humility of Eliot.

One reason why the old song is likely to be a very dangerous inspiration for the new Gaelic poet is that it is so difficult to separate its poetry from the mysteriously moving melodies that seem to rise spontaneously from the words. That the tunes do rise spontaneously, or that they and the words are simultaneous creations, is, I take it, the opinion of the greatest living authority, Mr William Matheson. When I put the matter to him, he said that of course they did rise spontaneously, and I don't think he misunderstood my words. The moral would seem to be that if a new Gaelic poet is more than ordinarily susceptible to music, he ought to avoid the old songs, just as Rilke, travelling through Switzerland, refused to see the Alps and drew down the blinds of his railway compartment. He was afraid that the Alps would disturb his art too much. The old songs are, however, human, as the Alps are not, and the modern poet can hardly shun them entirely. I think that the poet is safer in contemplating an art other than poetry if he cannot avoid 'impurities' that may come into his work from that of others, though the logic of such an insistence on purity would indicate that a poet should not read or hear, or have read or heard, any poetry but his own: this is the essence of D. H. Lawrences's theories but the very opposite of Eliot's.

No Gaelic poet, at all events, can shun the greatest glory of Gaelic poetry and make an artistic Origen of himself for the sake of his art. The old songs are 'there', and in a more human way than the mountains were 'there' in Mallory's words. If they are greater than poetry alone, nevertheless the poet cannot avoid them. It may be that there is the same kind of compulsion in the minds of the many who have maintained that if a poem cannot in some way approach the quality of music, if it lacks the lyrical cry, then it is not poetry; that even if it does not sing or chant, it must in some way suggest the song or chant. The question is how to find this suggestion of the song or chant in poetry that satisfies the mixed, troubled modern mind, and carries what is implicit in the old-fashioned phrase, 'criticism of life'. Perhaps, after all, the medley is the most satisfying modern poetic form. Perhaps, in spite of all Croce says, we must accept the 'unpoetic' flats out of which the lyrical peaks arise. Perhaps that is why so many good minds in Scotland consider MacDiarmid's *Drunk Man* and not *Sangschaw* the greatest single book of poetry by one man which has been produced in the British islands in this century. A few years ago I would have said *Sangschaw* myself, but now I am not sure. Probably no modern Gaelic poet will satisfy himself—even on the rare occasions when poets manage to do this—unless he has applied the lesson of the *Drunk Man*, or some similar lesson, as well as having drunk the heady wine of the old songs. A poet can disregard the internal combustion engine, but I doubt if he can disregard Freud and the atom bomb. Nevertheless, I feel that poetry will always resemble Valéry's sun:

> *Soleil, soleil, faute éclatantée,*
> *Tu gardes les coeurs de connaître*
> *Que l'univers n'est qu'un défaut*
> *Dans la pureté de non-être.*

What is in question is whether there can be poetry, or any art, which is fully relevant to the modern world and which at the same time satisfies the instinct for what is called 'beauty'. Psychoanalysis has shaken the belief in the wide divergence of good and bad, right and wrong, and has therefore undermined the basis of strong feeling which has seemed in the past to be essential to all art. Is an amoral delight no longer possible in serious art? Is George Campbell Hay's *Siubhal a' Choire* the kind of poem that ought to be no longer possible, and is Iain Crichton Smith's 'The Old Woman' the only kind of poem that ought now to be made? To me they are both fine poems, and both have strong feeling in them. George Campbell Hay's has an old delight, and Iain Crichton Smith's has the grey modern mind's profound sympathy for decrepit humanity. His old woman could be, though she is not, the symbol of a post-atomic world, but three out of four people would say that George Campbell Hay's poem is 'beautiful', while not more than one would say the same of Iain Crichton Smith's. Yeats excluded Wilfred Owen from his *Oxford Book of Modern Verse* because he felt that none of Owen's poems had in them what he called joy. By the same token he would have rejected 'The Old Woman'. Yeats, I am sure, was wrong about Owen. And I feel that the three out of four would be wrong about this particular poem of Iain Crichton Smith's.

135

# 9

## The Broken Heraldry

### by George Mackay Brown

Outwardly, the life of the Orkney people went on pretty much unaltered for about a thousand years, from the time of the Norse settlement until the mid-19th century. There were disturbances, upheavals, modifications: the change from Norse to Scottish overlordship in 1468; the Reformation; mass emigration to the colonies in the 19th century; and such minor indignities as the Cromwellian occupation and the press-gang during the Napoleonic wars—there were many Orkneymen at Trafalgar.

Lairds and presbyters come and go, but the backbone of a community is the farmer, and the pattern of labour remained virtually unchanged over that large span of time. Their daily work fashioned their outlook; what a man does and what he believes are closely interlinked. The Orkney crofters fitted into a hierarchy that had lasted so long that it seemed to be part of a natural as well as of a social order:

> The young laird,
> Seven fishermen with ploughs,
> Women, beasts, cornstalks, fish, stones.

The laird was the immediate head. Over all, unseen and omnipotent, was the King, and beyond him again, God.

The annual cycle of labour was fixed and unvarying: ploughing in winter, sowing and harrowing in spring, fishing and shearing and thatching in summer, harvesting in autumn. Then the long winter ritual of converting their corn into bread and ale—the flails, the quern-stones, the oven and the kirn. They lived in close communion with their beasts. Their houses were built low and long, like arks on the gentle swell of the hills, and like arks they held the mingled breathings of men and cattle under one roof. The crofter rarely left the parish he was born in. Once a year he took his family and beasts to the Lammas Fair in Kirkwall or Stromness. These fairs, along with christenings, weddings and funerals, were festive occasions: much gossip was exchanged by the women, great quantities of ale drunk by the men. Other times of high holiday were the Johnsmas Fires at midsummer and the Twelve Days of Christmas.

After Orkney passed from Norse to Scottish rule, and particularly after the Reformation, the Norn-speaking peasants were more and more mixed with immigrants from Scotland. Their own language died out, though it was still spoken in the 18th century in Harray and North Ronaldsay. Nowadays the people speak a diluted form of Scots (except for the 'proper' people, who use a genteel, insipid English) with Norwegian liltings and undertones.

The centre of the islands was the old town of Kirkwall, built around the 12th-century Cathedral of Saint Magnus the Martyr. Later, another town grew up on the other side of the main island—Stromness, a place of merchants and fishermen and whalers. The people were poor and heavily taxed, but in the 19th century, in common with the rest of Britain, in an access of fertility, they suddenly began to have large families. The islands overflowed with young people; there were constant streams of emigration. Young men saw little but bare tables at home, so they joined the Hudson's Bay Company as trappers, or went whaling all summer into the Arctic. A number of families settled in Leith and Glasgow. In 1901 a farmer called James Muir left Orkney for Glasgow with his wife, four sons and two daughters.

Meanwhile an important government measure was implemented—the Crofters Holdings (Scotland) Act of 1886. Hitherto the peasants had been almost completely at the mercy of their lairds. The degree of oppression varied from laird to laird: some of them were humane men, others were like General Borroughs of Rousay, whose exactions drove the Muir family from the island of Wyre. The Crofters Commission, set up after the Act, reduced rents substantially, wiped out arrears and laid down compensation for any improvements the crofters had carried out on their steadings. It was virtually the end of the lairds. The old mould was broken. As the decades passed, more and more crofters bought their holdings, and though a few lairds (mostly for the sake of prestige) continued to own this island and that estate, at some risk to their finances, the general pattern throughout Orkney now is for the farms and crofts to be owned by those who work them.

Change came rapidly at the turn of the century. The Orkney folk had got used to steamboats instead of sailing smacks, and to fairly regular communication between Leith and Orkney. Now they saw motor-cars for the first time, and almost at once they fell under a new enchantment. The young Orkneymen of today are experts with all kinds of gadgets and machines. Some farms are overloaded with tractors, far too heavily mechanised. The reek of petrol has overcome the immemorial smells of dung and sweat.

An old man told me about the inauguration of the motor-coach service between Stromness and Kirkwall early this century. On the first day the horse-coach ran too (it generally took three hours to cover the 15 miles to Kirkwall). In the motor-coach were the young, the daring and the modern; the horse-coach was full of old-fashioned, conservative, sceptical people. Horse-coach and motor-coach left at the same hour, and at once the horse-coach was left far behind. At Stenness the motor-coach broke down, and presently the mocking horse-coach passed it. But the engine was repaired and before Finstown the motor-coach, full of cheering 20th-century people, fumed and rattled past the patient horse-coach. Beyond Finstown it broke down again . . . But eventually the motor-coach reached Kirkwall first. It was the end of an old song.

One day in August 1914 crofters in the south isles of Orkney saw the strangest sight of their lives: enormous grey hulks looming out of the east between the islands and dropping anchor in Scapa Flow. The Royal Navy had entered its long-planned war base. There are plenty of stories of the sudden flood of prosperity that came to Orkney then: showers of silver rattling on counters, and shopkeepers literally shovelling their profits into sacks. (The stories are no doubt exaggerated—Orkneymen always improve a tale—but there is likely a kernel of truth in them.) Irish navvies came by the hundred to build camps and concrete defences, and had to pay grossly inflated prices for

138

chickens and draught port wine—whisky was unobtainable. In the middle of the war one Orkneyman happened to remark, tritely enough, that the Kaiser was everything that was bad and wicked. 'Na, na,' said an old lady whose shop was doing extra well, 'say not a word against the Kaiser. He's been a good Kaiser to us.'

The Second World War brought more huge transfusions of money and people. This time soldiers predominated; they ringed Scapa Flow with such a density of anti-aircraft fire and searchlights that the German bombers, after one or two forays early in the war, never came back. Servicemen of many countries were stationed in Orkney: the young women, used to their laconic suitors from the farms, never had such palaver and attention. Orkney was a bountiful place in these years. While the rest of Britain was gaunt with rationing, in the islands there seemed to be never-ending supplies of beef and eggs and cheese.

The Orkneyman in a romantic mood—and that is generally when he has a dram in him—likes to think that he stems from pure Norse stock, a Viking. Nothing could be further from the truth. The islands are a rich broth-pot of races. Pictish tribes lived along the lochs and shores long before the long-ships came out of the east. A mordant doctor said in a poem I wrote some years ago:

> First the aborigines
> That howked Skara Brae from the sand.
> Then the Picts,
> Those small dark cunning men
> Who scrawled their history in stone . . .
> And then the tigers from east over sea,
> The blond butchering Vikings,
> Whose last worry on sea or land
> Was purity of race, as they staggered
> couchwards
> After a fill of ale.
> Finally, to make the mixture thick and
> slab,
> The off-scourings of Scotland,
> The lowest sleaziest pimps from Lothian
> and the Mearns,

Fawning in the train of Black Pat,
And robbing and raping ad lib.

But that's not all.
For many a hundred ships have ripped their
    flanks
On Rora Head, or the Noup,
And Basque sailor lads and bearded skippers
    from Brittany
Left off their briny ways to cleave a furrow
Through Orkney crofts and lasses.

Not to speak of two world wars
And hordes of English and Yanks and
    Italians and Poles
Who took up their stations here:
By day the guns, by night the ancestral
    box-bed.
Only this morning I delivered a bairn
At Maggie o' Corsland's
With a subtle silk-selling Krishna smile.

A fine mixter-maxter!

But, satire or no, if you accept 'progress' as the mark of a
community's welfare, in the mid-20th century all seems to be
well with the Orkney people.

How was it with those crofters who had broken out of the
old unchanging way of life, who had left the islands? No record
remains of the fortunes of the Orkneyman forced from his
plough onto a man-of-war during the Napoleonic wars, but
the experience must have been terrifying. Hardly less strange,
and also unrecorded, was that of the young men who found
themselves among whales and icebergs, or trading for furs with
Indians in Baffin Bay. But we know what it was like for an
Orkney boy in Glasgow.

I walked to and from my work each day through a slum, for
there was no way of getting from the south side of Glasgow
to the city except through slums. These journeys filled me

with a sense of degradation: the crumbling houses, the twisted faces, the obscene words casually heard in passing, the ancient, haunting stench of pollution and decay, the arrogant women, the mean men, the terrible children, daunted me, and at last filled me with an immense blind dejection . . . My first years in Glasgow were wretched. The feeling of degradation continued, but it became more and more blind; I did not know what made me unhappy, nor that I had come into chaos. We had lived comfortably enough in Orkney, mainly on what we grew; but here everything had to be bought and paid for; there was so much money and so much food and clothes and warmth and accommodation to be had for it: that was all. This new state of things worried and perplexed my mother, and it gave each one of us a feeling of stringency which we had never known before . . . The first few years after we came to Glasgow were so stupidly wretched, such a meaningless waste of inherited virtue, that I cannot write of them even now without grief and anger. My father and mother felt lost because they were too old, and I because I was too young.

That is a unique account of the head-on clash between the pastoral and the industrial. The conflict broke Edwin Muir's life apart: for years he was unbearably unhappy, moving from office to office as a clerk, taking on a series of meaningless jobs which culminated in the Kafkaesque bone-factory at Greenock.

His marriage to Willa Anderson was the beginning of a long cure. The final salve was the discovery, at Hellerau in Germany, that he was a poet. The poems he wrote then came directly out of his Orkney childhood. He remembered, with terror and delight, the plough-horses on his father's farm.

> Their conquering hooves which trod the stubble down
> Were ritual that turned the field to brown,
> And their great hulks were seraphim of gold,
> Or mute ecstatic monsters on the mould.
>
> And oh the rapture when, one furrow done,
> They marched broad-breasted to the sinking sun!
> The light flowed off their bossy sides in flakes;
> The furrows rolled behind like struggling snakes,

This reaching back into the wholesome experiences of child-hood is very like Wordsworth. For Edwin Muir, as for Words-worth, the child in his natural setting moves in clouds of glory. And perhaps, now and then, because it meant so much to him, Edwin Muir tended to idealise life in the islands.

In 1934 he drove an old battered car through industrial and Highland Scotland, gathering material for his book, *Scottish Journey*. It was the period of the great depression. He was angered and saddened by what he saw everywhere—the aimless drift of the unemployed through the streets of ugly industrial towns, as if time had become a perpetual Sunday. He looked everywhere for a meaning: in the grotto of Carfin which the Catholic miners had built, in the old continuing courtesy of the Highlands. He crossed the Pentland Firth to Orkney. The tour-ist, he wrote,

will find a group of little islands, some quite flat, some hilly, all of them almost treeless, and all remarkably well and efficiently cultivated. He will also find a population of small farmers and crofters, naturally gentle and courteous in man-ners, but independent too, and almost all of them moderately prosperous. If he goes there in June, the long light, which never fades at that time of the year, but ebbs and ebbs until, before one can tell how, morning is there again, will charm and tease him . . . But he will not come to know much about the place unless he lives there for quite a long time, habitua-ting himself to the rhythm of the life, and training himself to be pleased with bareness and simplicity in all things . . . It is an agricultural community. The great majority of its farms are small and of a size that can be easily cultivated by the farmer and his family, without hiring outside labour. There are some large farms such as one finds in the south of Scotland and in England; but they are too few to affect the character of Orkney life, which is determined by these small, easily worked farms. Most of these farms are owned by their occupiers. In spite of their size, they are run on the most scientific modern lines; and this fact must be put to the credit of the Orkney people, who are unusually intelligent and adaptable; similar crofts in the Western Highlands and the Hebrides, for instance, are still cultivated as they were in past ages. At the same time the life of the people on these farms is, in its main lines, what it was 100 years ago. The farming community was poor then and is prosperous now; that is almost the sole difference.

Edwin Muir was too intelligent to confuse Orkney with Eden; Eden is a part of the heritage of every child. But he believed that an agricultural community lies closer to 'the fields of Paradise'. The life of an industrial city is subject to an uncontrollable cycle of booms and slumps, while a farming community exists within a clear pattern of labour and fulfilment—seed-time, reaping, the coupling of beasts, the harvest home, the gravestone.

Much has been written about the heraldic element in Edwin Muir—his preoccupations with emblems, shields, fabulous beasts. The fact is that the landscape of Orkney *looks* heraldic— hillsides quartered with tilth and pasture, beasts against the sky, the solitary falcon above the hill. Everywhere there is the feeling of timelessness that heraldry seeks to impose on the chaotic flux.

> Over the sound a ship so slow would pass
> That in the black hill's gloom it seemed to lie.
> The evening sound was smooth like sunken glass,
> And time seemed finished ere the ship passed by.

The carved devices over the laird's door, worn and enigmatic, have seen many lairds come and go, but the shield, outfacing death, insists that this family represents something of perdurable value. Death is not a negation of life but a completion and a celebration.

The scenery of Orkney as he remembered it dominated his imagination, and is worked into the texture and rhythms of his verse. It is a quiet landscape—low islands merging gently into one another, so that you can only distinguish one island from another by subtle tints and shadings. There are 'the great farm houses sunk in time', a church tower, a lighthouse, a slow passing ship on the horizon. The poetry mirrors the landscape exactly: there is the same even, unemphatic tone, the same dream-like clarity. After 400 years Orkney had found a poet at last.

All that wretched time in Glasgow, unknown to himself, he held the clue in his hand that was to lead him out of the labyrinth: it was the childhood he remembered, the natural and the fabulous and the supernatural collaborating in a single ceremony. Some critics say that Muir's poetry, crammed with symbols and archetypes, takes no account of the contemporary world. But he had lived too long in the heart of Europe between the wars not to know and care about what was happening in that world. Like all his best poetry, 'The Castle' is earth-rooted yet touched with the clarity of dreams. But it is also an exact parable of the defeat of France in 1940. Of course, the poem is about more than that: he is remembering the tumble of stones in Wyre, where he played as a small boy, imagining how that Viking castle fell, unweaving the story, weaving the fable. Into the complete web are woven Kolbein Hruga of Wyre, General Gamelin of the Maginot Line, and the whole human race—for essentially it is a story of the Fall.

I have said that his view of life in the Orkneys in the mid-Thirties is in some ways idealised. The remembered Eden of childhood, the contrast with the depressed industrial areas of Scotland, made it appear better than it was. Now, 30 years later, he would have found the Orcadians more prosperous than ever —affluence in the towns, in the countryside marshland drained and ploughed and new patches of cultivation on every barren hillside, cars and television masts everywhere. It would be rather complacent, all the same, to believe that all is well with the islands. Formerly a people of strongly-marked individuality, the Orcadians are gradually losing their identity—or rather they have willingly merged their identity with the rest of the western world. Many things contribute to this loss: wireless and television, compulsory education, newspapers, the insidious notion that urban ways of life are necessarily superior to rural ways. A town like Stromness, even 30 years ago, used to be alive with 'characters', the kind of delightfully surrealistic folk you read about in Russian novels. There are less and less of them now. It is as if people were ashamed to be different from one another.

One senses a growing coldness—the coldness of people who have received the fatal blessing of prosperity. The old gentle courtesy of country people, though it exists, is no longer so apparent; nor are the simple natural services they used to render each other in the harvest fields; nor is the gathering together in houses for fiddle-music and story-telling in the winter.

This break-up, though it has accelerated of late years, has been going on for a very long time, before Edwin Muir was born, before the first paddle-ship churned its way across the Pentland Firth. The fissure reaches far back through many generations to the Reformation. It was then that the old heraldry began to crack, that the idea of 'progress' took root in men's minds. What was broken, irremediably, in the 16th century was the fullness of life of a community, its single interwoven identity. In earlier times the temporal and the eternal, the story and the fable, were not divorced, as they came to be after Knox: they used the same language and imagery, so that the whole of life was illuminated. Crofters and fishermen knew what Christ was talking about, better perhaps than the canons and prebendaries of St Magnus, because they bore the stigmata of labour on their bodies—the net let down into the sea, the sower going forth to sow, the fields white towards harvest. The miracle of the five loaves and two fishes must have been intensely meaningful to a people who, in spite of perennial poverty and occasional famine, saw the bannock and the salt on their winter table. Most marvellous of all was that their daily labours were a divine image for their strivings heavenwards, and were rewarded at last by the Bread of Heaven, the Blessed Sacrament, Christ himself dwelling in them. Here was the ultimate intermingling of the earthy and the holy. They saw it as the superlative wit and charity of Heaven.

They were sustained by an immense confidence and security. Ultimately all was well with them. They knew that an angel and a devil wrestled inside each of them for possession of their soul, and the outcome was uncertain until the moment of death. But the sacraments of the Church, particularly penance and the Eucharist, were an infallible remedy. Grey mediocre people that they were, they believed that a shining thread of immortality was ravelled through them. Poor people, they were yet lords and princes with heavenly treasures lying thick about them. These beliefs gave their lives gaiety and confidence, and this gaiety is expressed in the ballads and songs that have come down to us. There, earthiness and blessedness are inextricably merged.

Be ye maids or be ye nane,
We're a' Saint Mary's men,

Ye's a' be kissed or we gang hame,
Fore wur Lady.

Suddenly the violent change to Calvinism was thrust on them.
Their sacraments were forbidden and squandered; their altars
and images put down; black preachers solemnly impressed on
them that their strivings towards the consummation of heaven
would avail them nothing, since either their salvation or their
damnation was sealed before the beginning of the world. From
that time on incarnate angels and demons toiled in the fields,
and the estate of 'dear and dogged man' was broken up and
refashioned. Innocence gave place to a dark, brooding awareness. The Orcadians have always been a religious people, and it
is more than possible that religion gone sour has contributed to
the striking incidence of mental trouble in the islands over the
last few centuries. From that time, too, the old music and poetry
died out, because the single vision which is the source of all art
had been choked. Poets followed priests into the darkness.

It is almost impossible, at a distance of four centuries, to
estimate the catastrophe that Calvinism brought to Orkney (and
to the rest of Scotland). Many recorded instances survive of men,
six or seven generations later, taking their troubles and sickness
to the ruins of some pre-Reformation chapel, praying there, and
leaving offerings among the stones. Parish ministers inveighed
against this so often and so sternly that the practice must have
been common right up to the end of the 18th century.

Much, of course, remained. Though their interior lives had
been remoulded, the Orkney crofters and fishermen still lived
close to the sources from which they gathered their food. Their
lives, at best, kept the dignity and austerity of the Wordsworth-
ian peasant, mingled with the bawdry of Burnsian peasants (but
the bawdry was reserved for the smithy and the stable and the
horsemen's rituals), and with not a little of the sentimentality of
those in whom flesh and spirit have been unravelled. Occasionally, on this island or that, awesome things happened. Some
evangelist would arrive and convince the people of their sins.
This is what happened on Sanday in the year 1860, as told by
the Reverend John Paul of Kirkwall.

A portion of Scripture was about to be read, and in introduc-
ing the subject, the name of Jesus was mentioned, when a
146

young man who had been deeply impressed, and who was sitting before the pulpit, started up, and stretching out his arms, and looking eagerly in the direction in which he pointed, cried out in ecstasy—'Jesus! Jesus! see Him! see Him! He is glorious in holiness! He is the chief among ten thousand! He is altogether lovely!' And, turning to the audience, he proceeded with great fluency and power to speak of Jesus' suitableness as a Saviour for sinners. But his voice, although a stentorian one, was soon devoured by a tremendous outburst of feeling —piercing cries of agony—loud exclamations of joy—prayers uttered audibly, and with great earnestness.

It is almost certain that some of Edwin Muir's ancestors were involved in these scenes, for the Muirs came from Sanday. He himself inherited some of this primitive evangelism: once in his boyhood and again in Glasgow he knelt among the elect at the penitent form, though the conversions were not lasting. He gave the sweetest and noblest expression to this stark fundamentalism in 'The Transfiguration'.

> So from the ground we felt that virtue branch
> Through all our veins till we were whole, our wrists
> As fresh and pure as water from a well,
> Our hands made new to handle holy things,
> The source of all our seeing rinsed and cleansed
> Till earth and light and water entering there
> Gave back to us the clear unfallen world.
> We would have thrown our clothes away for lightness,
> But that even they, though sour and travel-stained,
> Seemed, like our flesh, made of immortal substance,
> And the soiled flax and wool lay light upon us
> Like friendly wonders, flower and flock entwined
> As in a morning field.

This is how the world must have looked to the elect kneeling at the penitent form. But one guesses that St Francis among the birds and St Magnus among the swords were touched by the same glory. 'The Transfiguration' is more than Calvinist or Catholic: it is perennial Christianity.

Like most of Scotland's writers in this century, Muir came to resent bitterly what Calvinism had done to the country. His was the first great poetry to come out of Orkney since the Reformation, and he did much to bring together the broken pieces of our heritage and to fit some of them together into a meaningful whole. To do so, he had to leave some things out. Though he gave us a magnificent portrait of his cousin Sutherland in *An Autobiography*, he never succeeded in gathering that lewd, earthy peasant into his poetry.

It is hard to see what the future of Orkney will be. Farmers and shopkeepers and tradespeople (the fishermen not so certainly) have secure lives. But the tide of history is moving against all remote agricultural communities and, year by year, is depopulating the islands. There comes a time when a small island ceases to be viable: when only, say, five or six families are left out of a score. The authorities step in with an expensive pier, and the remaining families find the pier useful for flitting out their beasts and furniture and tractors; and, like Stroma, the island is deserted for ever. In Rackwick on the island of Hoy, a beautiful, fertile valley that lies between the hills and the Pentland Firth, only one farm is left out of 15 or 16; the hill slopes are strewn with roofless crofts. I have written a kind of elegy for Rackwick, called 'Dead Fires'.

At Burnmouth the door hangs from a broken hinge
And the fire is out.

The windows of Shore empty sockets
And the hearth coldness.

At Bunertoon the small drains are choked.
Thrushes nest in the chimney.

Stars shine through the roofbeams of Scar.
No flame is needed
To warm ghosts and nettles and rats.

Greenhill is sunk in a new bog.
No kneeling woman
Blows red wind though squares of ancient bog.

The Moss is a tumble of stones.
That black stone
Is the stone where the hearth-fire was rooted.

And in Midhouse among those flowers of flame
Bread and fish were baked.
That enchanted stone turned the blue lobster red.

In Crowsnest the sunken hearth
Was an altar for priests of legend,
Old seamen from the clippers with silken beards.

The three-toe'd pot at the wall of Park
Is lost to women's cunning.
A slow fire of rust eats the cold iron.

The sheep drift through Reuming all winter.
Sheep and snow
Blanch fleetingly the black stone.

It is still there,
The flat stone in Windbrake where the water-pot stood,
But always the eye seeks the charred stone.

From that sacred stone the children of the valley
Drifted lovewords
And out of labour to the lettered kirkyard stone.

The fire beat like a heart in each house
From the first corner-stone
Till they led through the sagging lintel the last old ones.

The poor and the good fires are all quenched.
Now, cold angel, keep the valley
From the bedlam and cinders of a Black Pentecost.

But there is a more serious threat than depopulation—the
threat of a break-down in community. Perhaps this break-down
is inevitable once the heraldic vision that holds a people together is shattered. The great paradox of our time in Orkney is

that with increased prosperity and education and communications, the quality of life has grown progressively poorer.
Whereas the medieval Orkney peasant lived among treasures of
legend and faith, we stand like exiles among accumulations of
expensive trash. Once more, unknown to us, the Castle has been
silently breached.

Perhaps something we cannot imagine will flower out of this
desolation; it may be that out of some total destruction a kind
of resurrection will come. Edwin Muir imagined, in one of his
poems, an atomic holocaust, and after it, the plough-horses of
his childhood returning.

> Barely a twelvemonth after
> The seven-day war that put the world to sleep,
> Late in the evening the strange horses came . . .

# 10

# What Images Return

## by Muriel Spark

A few years ago I was obliged to spend some weeks in the North British Hotel in Edinburgh, isolated and saddened by many things, while my father's last illness ran its course in the Royal Infirmary. It was necessary for me to be within call. I do not like the public rooms and plushy lounges of hotels anywhere in the world, I do not sit in them; and least of all in one's native city is it spiritually becoming to sit in the lounges of big hotels.

I spent most of my time in my room waiting for the hours of visiting my father to come round. I think at such times in one's life one tends to look out of the window oftener and longer than usual. I left my work and my books and spent my time at the window. It was a high, wide window, with an inside ledge, broad and long enough for me to sit in comfortably with my legs stretched out. The days before Easter were suddenly warm and sunny. From where I sat propped in the open window frame, I could look straight onto Arthur's Seat and the Salisbury Crags, its girdle. When I sat the other way round I could see part of the Old City, the east corner of Princes Street Gardens, and the black Castle Rock. In those days I experienced an in-pouring of love for the place of my birth, which I am aware was psychologically connected with my love for my father and with the exiled sensation of occupying a hotel room which was really meant for strangers.

Edinburgh is the place that I, a constitutional exile, am essentially exiled from. I spent the first 18 years of my life, during the 1920s and 1930s there. It was Edinburgh that bred within me the conditions of exiledom; and what have I been doing since then but moving from exile into exile? It has ceased to be a fate, it has become a calling.

151

My frequent visits to Edinburgh for a few weeks at a time throughout the years have been the visits of an exile in heart and mind—cautious, affectionate, critical. It is a place where I could not hope to be understood. The only sons and daughters of Edinburgh with whom I can find a common understanding are exiles like myself. By exiles I do not mean Edinburgh-born members of Caledonian Societies. I do not consort in fellowship with the Edinburgh natives abroad merely on the Edinburgh basis. It is precisely the Caledonian Society aspect of Edinburgh which cannot accommodate me as an adult person.

Nevertheless, it is the place where I was first understood. James Gillespie's Girls' School, set in solid state among the green meadows, showed an energetic faith in my literary life. I was the school's Poet and Dreamer, with appropriate per-quisites and concessions. I took this for granted, and have never since quite accustomed myself to the world's indifference to art and the process of art, and to the special needs of the artist.

I have started the preceding paragraph with the word 'never-theless' and am reminded how my whole education, in and out of school, seemed even then to pivot around this word. I was aware of its frequent use. My teachers used it a great deal. All grades of society constructed sentences bridged by 'neverthe-less'. It would need a scientific study to ascertain whether the word was truly employed more frequently in Edinburgh at the time than anywhere else. It is my own instinct to associate the word, as the core of a thought-pattern, with Edinburgh par-ticularly. I can see the lips of tough elderly women in musquash coats taking tea at MacVittie's, enunciating this word of final justification, I can see the exact gesture of head and chin and gleam of the eye that accompanied it. The sound was roughly 'niverthelace' and the emphasis was a heartfelt one. I believe myself to be fairly indoctrinated by the habit of thought which calls for this word. In fact I approve of the ceremonious ac-cumulation of weather forecasts and barometer-readings that pronounce for a fine day, before letting rip on the statement: 'Nevertheless, it's raining.' I find that much of my literary composition is based on the nevertheless idea. I act upon it. It was on the nevertheless principle that I turned Catholic.

It is impossible to know how much one gets from one's early

environment by way of a distinctive character, or whether for better or worse. I think the puritanical strain of the Edinburgh ethos is inescapable, but this is not necessarily a bad thing. In the south of England the puritanical virtues tend to be regarded as quaint eccentricities—industriousness, for instance, or a horror of debt. A polite reticence about sex is often mistaken for repressions. On the other hand, spiritual joy does not come in an easy consistent flow to the puritanically-nurtured soul. Myself, I have had to put up a psychological fight for my spiritual joy.

Most Edinburgh-born people, of my generation at least, must have been brought up with a sense of civic superiority. We were definitely given to understand that we were citizens of no mean city. In time, and with experience of other cities, one would have discovered the beautiful uniqueness of Edinburgh for oneself as the visitors do. But the physical features of the place surely had an effect as special as themselves on the outlook of the people. The Castle Rock is something, rising up as it does from pre-history between the formal grace of the New Town and the noble network of the Old. To have a great primitive black crag rising up in the middle of populated streets of commerce, stately squares and winding closes, is like the statement of an unmitigated fact preceded by 'nevertheless'. In my time the society existing around it generally regarded the government and bureaucracy of Whitehall as just a bit ridiculous. The influence of a place varies according to the individual. I imbibed, through no particular mentor, but just by breathing the informed air of the place, its haughty and remote anarchism. I can never now suffer from a shattered faith in politics and politicians, because I never had any.

When the shrill telephone in my hotel room woke me at four in the morning, and a nurse told me that my father was dead, I noticed, with that particular disconnected concentration of the fuddled mind, that the rock and its castle loomed as usual in the early light. I noted this, as if one might have expected otherwise.

153

# 11

## Borderlines

### by Alastair Reid

I write of Scotland with that most doubtful of all qualifications
—20 years and the most changeable part of my life away from
it, not just away but involved in a slew of other countries and
contexts, the United States for a stretch, Europe, Spain, Latin
America and, in particular, the Spanish language, so that I have
changed not only my skin but all my spots and tartans; and yet,
I don't think that I have let more than 18 months ever pass
without going back to Scotland. This in no sense means that
I was not able to stay away, but only that, with distance, Scotland became more and more incredible to me, and I had to
return to verify it, if you like—that, and to have a whiff of the
growing landscape, since I was born and bred there, and childhood landscapes are irreplaceable. My feelings about Scotland
now all come from a distance which is not just geographical; I
would never live there again.

I am attached to different parts of Scotland in different ways
—to Galloway and the Isle of Arran almost mystically, for it
was there that I experienced all the epiphanies of dawning consciousness, which have little to do with other people, but everything to do with one's own being. In a sense, I carry these two
landscapes inside me like secrets, and revisit them in awe and
trepidation, for private and personal reasons. They recur un-
expectedly in poems, in dreams, in occasional visions, and they
continue durably inside me, safe from reality. I am connected
to St Andrews, that placid centre of non-learning, where I
spent student years, insulated from everything outside, finding
out what I had to find out. St Andrews smacks always of holiday,
of leisure, a place for hobbyists and librarians, and if I ever
believed that retirement were possible, or even desirable, it would

be high on my list of limbos. But it was in the Borders that I *lived*, for a ten-year stretch, so that, from my Scottish past, the Borders were real life, for better or for worse. I doubt whether I would have chosen to live there, but then, to choose where one wants to live is a supreme luxury, and takes work. The Borders —and the town of Selkirk in particular—was my fate.

When you leave places far enough behind, they take a certain shape in the memory, something like a design on wallpaper. The Borders loom in my mind as a small archipelago of stony towns in a placid sea of grass, woods and furrows, small, bristling islands in a state of armed truce with one another, with their village satellites, their lumbering bus-ferries, their pugnacious localisms. I read them as a miniature nation of borough-states, each town with its distinct character: Hawick the most successfully self-contained, swashbuckling, burly, meaning business, Melrose quiescent, genteel, semi-retired, bucolic, Selkirk serious but sad, aggressively defensive, Kelso elegant, even snooty, self-superior, Galashiels dismal and matter-of-fact, uninspired and uninspiring—on and on, as one peels their strange substance, like varieties of onion. Whatever their rivalries— and they are intense and scathing—the Border towns are solidly united against 'foreigners' and present an implacable front to criticism and dissent from all quarters. There was a famous Selkirk worthy who proclaimed staunchily that 'a day oot o' Selkirk was a day wasted'; what's more, he believed it, and was often invoked prophetically.

Hugh MacDiarmid's evocation of his Border growing-up, which accompanies me in this book, brings sharp shocks of recognition, for similarly I spent as much time as possible out of doors, on the run, rampaging through the seasons, getting away with as much as possible, mindlessly delighted. We were foreigners, sure enough, coming from the west, but it was only when the Common Riding came round that this became vaguely troubling—I was not a Soutar, and hence automatically disqualified from holding local office, a privileged spectator at best. Even so, this was not at all tormenting, because I was already aware of alternatives to Selkirk—Whithorn, which we had left behind and sometimes revisited, Arran, to which we made an annual pilgrimage, a few visiting family friends who smacked of other worlds, and vague dreams of foreign parts, with which I

comforted my occasional disquiets. I had curiosity but no am-
bition, but I assumed, on a scarcely conscious level, that I was
going to leave Selkirk somewhere along the line. My secret hero
was a vague uncle, who turned up only twice in my life, but
who had lived in the Cocos Islands, and filled my ears with such
towering stories in the course of one small walk that my fantasy
and my present life were divided for ever after. Alienation set
in early but unresentfully. It did not trouble my mind. As
members of a minister's family, we were supposed, in the eyes of
the town, to be, if not morally impeccable, at least small mis-
sionaries of obedience; but this, rather than loading me with
intolerable burdens of guilt, inspired me to confound my
cronies by being more outrageous than they were, and to per-
plex my teachers by deliberately not coming up to their expecta-
tions. Looking back, I think I enjoyed both Selkirk and my
secret life, although I began to cultivate a conscious disrespect
for the place.

The aura hanging over the Border towns, I think more formidably fierce there than anywhere I can think of, is that of
permanence—to be more specific, a permanence of mind.
Change takes the form of tearing down one house and building
another, closing one shop and opening it under new management, but change in any attitudinal sense is not just resisted—
it is unthinkable. I have seen much more primitive villages in
Spain wrestle stoutly with change and yield to it without losing
their souls, but I doubt that the Border towns would take it in
even were it to happen, even although it has happened. I never
returned much to Selkirk, mainly because, the few times I did,
I was granted no reality other than a retrospective one—the
channels of communication were no longer open. ('You've been
Away'—the relentless Scottish gambit for dealing with strays
who return, full of seditious experience, comparative judgments
and disquieting tales, followed as it always is by a patient catalogue of local births, marriages, deaths and disasters.) I have
puzzled over this blunt lack of curiosity, and concluded that it is
at best defensive, in the sense that, if you have accepted a locality
profoundly, all alternatives are dangerous by definition. The
intractability of the Border towns is even fiercer than that—
they refuse to consider alternatives to their own imperfectly
understood way of life, to which they have surrendered their

separateness as human beings: so that in the Borders, there are few questions, only simple, declarative statements, most of them imperatives. I felt, and still feel, of the Border towns that they have something approaching a collective consciousness, baffling in its unanimity, and that individual differences, although they abound eccentrically, are rarely differences of attitude and conviction. The Borders are a way of life that expects acquiescence and does not brook contradiction, yet all this implicitly, for the Borders are anything but self-conscious, and never talk of themselves except in pawky clichés of self-congratulation. When I was innocent of speech and thought, I had no quarrel with the place at all, and revelled in the countryside and even in the taciturnity of the town, which made its rules for behaviour indelibly felt beyond words. But it was when words began in me, and the stirrings of a separate consciousness, that I began to separate myself from the community and look for the few people I could find who said things I could not expect, and who would answer questions rather than brush them aside. So I never belonged to the Borders at any point at all, and never really communicated with them, even when I wanted to desperately.

This non-communication, this deliberate inarticulateness, exists in Scotland like a wall. Some vital thread between inner realisation and outward expression seems to have been severed for ever, but voluntarily and even thankfully. When I go back to Scotland now, I find myself eavesdropping in disbelief at conversations which sound like formal models in phrase-books, exchanges on the street which seem to have been scripted in stone, so predictable are they. This is nowhere more stolidly true than in the Borders. Going back now, I meet people with whom I shared some part of the past, and our conversations circle warily, and usually end up invoking an incident I have forgotten, or retracing people I vaguely remember who are defined only by what has befallen them, or cataloguing accounts of local disasters. These conversations obviously cannot last long, and sooner or later reach that plateau of uncomfortable, grunt-punctuated silence which Borderers seem to inhabit most of the time. Communing with their thoughts? I wish I believed that to be anything more than a novelist's euphuism for vacancy of mind. I wish I could feel that Borderers regard their private feelings as something too hallowed for utterance. But even when they cut loose, stumbling and ranting with drink, there is no great break-through, but instead a rumble of anecdote, an aggressive petulance, a steady suspicious girning or a sentimental wallow, but no trace of the turbulent private self which might be expected to show even a furtive face. Whether from a collective guilt or fear or shame, the private self gets irretrievably buried, and the few who prevail are labelled as eccentrics or 'characters' and granted licences which allow them to be at once outrageous but ineffectual, the stuff of fresh anecdote. When I look back on the characters who speckled my childhood, I see that they must have been either stark staring mad or at least miserably unhappy. Spontaneity is immediately suspicious, private feelings a cause for shame; one is still told, by people wearing pain on their faces: 'Oh, we can't complain.'

Whatever it stems from—the Protestant ethic, pride, guilt, the fear of being found out, the notion of human life as something to be tholed and endured—this inborn attitude seems to me intolerable, unfruitful and certainly unfulfilling. More oppressively, it is unassailable: no Borderer I know, except for a few local cynics who have already thrown their own respectability cheerfully away, will admit to a state of affairs which he understands only imperfectly, nor will any ex-Borderer who has liberated himself consider the effort worth making. Moreover, there is really nothing wrong—no one, by analogy, is an alcoholic until his own misery drives him to admit the fact to himself; and I certainly feel no evangelist's zeal where the Borders are concerned, nor do I expect any latter-day Ataturk to storm through these flinty towns, tearing aside veils, bedclothes and lace curtains. But if Scotland is to have an autonomous future of any kind, the problem will be much less one of being granted freedoms of choice than one of thinking clearly and making choices—freedom to what end? If all decisions have to achieve the lowest common denominator of unanimity, then they will not really be decisions at all; and the opinions I hear voiced in the Borders are opinions expecting a confirming Aye, rather than the risk of an exchange, which means that candidates for any office are expected to confirm and please rather than to convince—the only individual right exercised is the right to reject.

It was not until I lived in Spain that I began to think at all about the relation of language and communication to national character; but now I find it difficult to disentangle them. I found that, when I had learned the Spanish language with some degree of fluency, I had grown another self quite unlike my Scottish one, a self that was much more spontaneous and exuberant and one which allowed me to get angry and gesticulate, to put my moods into words. It was a liberation that had, of course, already taken place, but what I did find was that the Spanish language fitted me easily and agreeably, and opened to me wavelengths of exchange which seemed natural and unequivocal. Spaniards are aggressively and vociferously individual, without lacking courtesy or formality; moreover, they imbue everything with their own moods, and are comically frank about themselves. The physicality of Spain and the Mediterranean shone through, with the result that, when I went back to the Borders from Spain, old habits of not saying sat less easily on me than ever. The sense of life as fate is, if anything, stronger in Spain than it is in Scotland, but the reaction to it could not be more different: no silent, long-suffering stoical acceptance but a ribald, robust blowing-off of steam, a mocking self-dramatisation that restores equilibrium, and shakes a wordy fist at the air. More than that, once I had moved into another language, language ceased to be an absolute, as it must, and I became inevitably more aware of ways of saying, over and above what was said, and of language and language habits as ways of being. Though no one language is superior to any other, there are bound to be comparisons, and my Spanish experience took me back to listening again in disbelief to the language mannerisms of the Borders as a kind of behaviour, for there, language is used to conceal rather than to clarify.

The language is rich enough, no question. It flowers in anecdote, in particularities, in intimacy (if Scots poetry has any dominant characteristic, it is that of putting itself on intimate terms with everything it touches). There is a fund of eccentric and hilarious anecdote, certainly, and a story for every occasion and situation—but this bottomless fund of instance and example hardly constitutes thought, nor serves as much of a substitute. But somewhere along the line, a vital connection gets lost, the connection through which people keep language as a way of putting *themselves* into words. Borderers especially seem always suspicious of any linguistic agility in others, of 'fine talk', of any way of talking which is not exactly in accord with theirs. Their own way with language is to offer up phrases which invite agreement, to affirm one another—the constructions are tentative, expecting reassurance. 'You'll be glad to be back, you'll be staying for a while?' It seems almost brutal to counter them with the truth. Borderers are all instinctive custodians of a *status quo*, protective towards themselves and one another, censorious according to a public morality which they maintain ruthlessly but understand only imperfectly: it makes them at worst into fearsome gossips, at best into wary nay-sayers with an infallible eye for the flaws in any argument. Even more, it makes them extremely difficult to identify as individual people. Ask who someone is, and you will be given a catalogue in reply, of family connection, of employment, of memorable feats, of external idiosyncrasies, but nothing more—nothing which might come from insight or observation or personal judgment. It is as though all the human characteristics we associate with 'personality' and an inner life just did not exist. In short, what always perplexes me about the Scots as a vague generality, and about the Borders in overwhelming particularity, is the almost complete absence of the analytical dimension, the capacity to see *into* oneself and other people. Judgment is instinctive, not the result of thought; an individual is less a separate entity than a function within a community; people have meaning, not in themselves, but in a context.

I write this less as a grouse than as a bewilderment, for I find it difficult to understand any life without this dimension, yet in the Borders it does go on, with a minimum of self-concern, with an almost complete acceptance. Repressed? Unquestionably; but unhappy? Much harder to answer, in a human climate where to claim unhappiness, to look for change, would seem no more than indulgences. There is a sense in which the Scots would consider themselves as Scots before they thought of themselves as human beings, since Scotland provides their entire frame of reference, and alternatives, even if they exist, are rejected out of hand. To grow into the Borders is to have the mind slowly close, and to assume the collective mentality without much question, and certainly without pain. There is no loyal opposition, no generational rebellion—the only alternative to accepting completely is to leave. Even now, when there are signs of economic death in the air, falling populations and a faltering prosperity, this is taken in less as a situation to be remedied than as a different turn of fate, a new shape of cross. The salvation lies in that gloomy humour, the 'could be warse' strain which precludes anything getting better except by accident, the complete absence of joy.

In the last analysis, I may just be talking about a personal perplexity, the difficulty of equating two totally separate parts of myself, or two separate selves. Except that I know that my discontents always stem from a lack of clarity, and that I resist the closed mind with ferocity. I am at war with the Border mentality in myself, victim and liberator, and the only relief is in clarity, and in open lines of communication. It seems to me that the first reaction of any child who has regretted the lack of communication with his parents would be to make sure that his own children would not suffer the same lack; yet in the Borders, the same uncomprehending silence sets in between the generations, and the sense of permanence obliterates any need for change. I can remember coming bursting in from just having glimpsed eternity in a grain of sand and being told, curtly: 'Your tea's cold.' It may be that tea is the reality and glimpses of eternity only a temporary foolishness. If I ever thought so, it might be possible to give up resisting and to belong.

I overstate my case deliberately, because the Borders are themselves an exaggeration of their own private attitudes; nevertheless, those separate-minded individuals have been unable to dent the façade of the collective attitude. I am trying to state a disquiet, generally, and my argument either clarifies a situation not usually realised, or must be rejected out of hand. If I were a Borderer, I would take rejection as confirmation, and nod smugly. There is a sense in which the Scots are never wrong about anything, which, translated, means that they shut from their minds any thought of an alternative to their own way of life. National infallibility is not anything to admire, although its persistence into this turbulent present may be admirable, as were kamikaze pilots in the Pacific. But with Scotland on the edge of gaining some form of self-decision, that blind conviction looks like promising disaster and confusion rather than health. It is also less important to understand how and why these attitudes have come about than the simple fact that they exist, and that they are limitations rather than assets, that they are something like a national neurosis. That things could be worse is a woeful substitute for the hope that they could be better; that human life is bearable seems to me to fall miserably short of the possibility of its being fruitfully enjoyed.

# 12

## Growing Up in Langholm

### by Hugh MacDiarmid

After journeying over most of Scotland, England and central, southern and eastern Europe, as well as America, Siberia and China, I am of the opinion that 'my native place'—the Muckle Toon of Langholm, in Dumfriesshire—is the bonniest place I know: by virtue not of the little burgh in itself (though that has its treasurable aspects, and on nights when, as boys, we used to thread its dim streets playing 'Jock, Shine the Light', and race over the one bridge, past the factory, and over the other, with the lamp reflections wriggling like eels at intervals in the racing water, had an indubitable magic of its own), but by virtue of the wonderful variety and quality of the scenery in which it is set. The delights of sledging on the Lamb Hill or Murtholm Brae; of gathering hines in the Langfall; of going through the fields of Baggara hedged in honeysuckle and wild roses, through knee-deep meadow-sweet to the Scrog Nut Wood and gathering the nuts or crab-apples there; of blaeberrying on Warblaw or the Castle Hill; of dookin' and guddlin' or making islands in the Esk or Ewes or Wauchope and lighting stick fires on them and cooking potatoes in tin cans—these are only a few of the joys I knew, in addition to the general ones of hill-climbing and penetrating the five glens which (each with its distinct character) converge upon or encircle the town—Eskdale, Wauchopedale, Tarrasdale, Ewesdale and, below the town Carlislewards, the Dean Banks.

As we grew up, too, we learned to savour the particular qualities and rites of Langholm in comparison with other Border burghs: the joys of Langholm Common Riding compared with those at Selkirk or Hawick, for example; the peculiar shibboleths of local pronunciation; the historical

163

associations of our corner of the 'Ballad-land' rife with its tales of raidings and reivings and with the remnants of peels; the wealth of local 'characters' who were still about.

As I grew into my early teens I ranged further afield, and soon all the Borders were within my ken. Many places had their special beauties or points of interest and advantage; but none had the variety of beauty centred round Langholm itself—none seemed so complete a microcosm of the entire Borderland. I knew where to find not only the common delights of hill and forest and waterside (and chiefest of all these to me were the chestnut trees at the sawmill—even now it thrills me to remember the beautiful chestnuts, large and luxurious as horses' eyes, which so surprisingly displayed themselves when we cracked open the prickly green shells, and I remember many huge strops of them I strung and many a fierce competition at Conquerors), but also the various kinds of orchises, and butterwort, sundew, and the like; the various nests—including Terrona crags where ravens nested; how to deal with adders and smoke out wasps' 'bikes', and much other lore of that sort. In short, a boyhood full of country sights and sounds—healthy and happy and able to satisfy its hunger with juicy slices of a big yellow neep stolen from an adjoining field.

I never made any conscious decision that I should be a writer. That was a foregone conclusion from my very early life. I don't know if it originated with myself. When I was nine or ten my teachers seemed to realise that writing was going to be my destiny and I may have absorbed the idea from them. Certainly from a very early age I had begun to try to write for the local paper at Langholm, where my father was the local postman. We lived in the Post Office buildings. The library, the nucleus of which had been left by Thomas Telford, the famous engineer, was upstairs. I had access to it, and used to fill a big washing-basket with books and bring it downstairs as often as I wanted to. There were upwards of 12,000 books in the library, and a fair number of new books, chiefly novels, was constantly bought. Before I left home (when I was 14) I could go up into that library in the dark and find any book I wanted. I read almost every one of them.

My grandfather, John Grieve, was a power-loom tuner in a Langholm tweed mill. I only remember seeing him once—

shortly before he died, when I was about four years old. An alert 'jokey' little man, I remember he wore a transparent, butter-coloured waistcoat or linen jacket; and on the occasion I recall I caught him in the act of taking some medicine of a vivid red colour, and somehow or other got it into my childish head that he was drinking blood, and thought of him with horror—not unmixed with envy—for years afterwards. I resemble him physically (in point of leanness and agility, though I am con-siderably taller) and facially (a big brow and all the features squeezed into the lower half of my face); but when I was a lad the older folk used to tell me I took after him in another re-spect: 'just like your grandfaither,' they used to say, 'aye amang the lassies.' As boys my brother and I wore the Graham tartan. Our mother was Elizabeth Graham. If my father's people were mill-workers in the little Border burghs, my mother's people were agricultural workers. My alignment from as early as I can remember was almost wholly on the side of the industrial workers and not the rural people. I have never had anything but hatred and opposition for deproletarianising and back-to-the-land schemes; my faith has always been in the industrial workers and the growth of the third factor between man and nature—the machine. But even as a boy, from the steadings and cot-tages of my mother's folk and their neighbours in Wauchope and Eskdalemuir and Middlebie and Dalbeattie and Tunder-garth, I drew the assurance that I felt and understood the spirit of Scotland and the Scottish folk in no common measure, and that that made it possible that I would in due course become a great national poet of Scotland. My mother's people lie in the queer old churchyard of Crowdieknowe in the parish of Middle-bie.

There was certainly nothing 'lowering', in Lawrence's sense of the word, in Border life when I was a boy. Langholm was full of genial ruffians like the employer to whom, communist though I am, I look back with the utmost relish, who, after carefully instructing a workman whom he was sending up Westerkirk way as to what he was to do, ended: 'and just call in when you come back and I'll gie you the sack!' Border life was raw, vigorous, rich, bawdy, and the true test of my own work is the measure in which it has recaptured something of that unquenchable humour, biting satire, profound wisdom cloaked in bantering gaiety, and the wealth of mad humour, with not a trace of whimsy, in the general leaping, light-hearted, reckless assault upon the conventions of dull respectability.

My first introduction to my native land was when my mother wrapped me well in a Shetland shawl and took me to the door to see—but, alas, my infant eyesight could not carry so far, nor if it could have seen would my infant brain have understood —the most unusual sight of the Esk frozen over so hard that carts and horses could go upon it for 20 miles as upon a road and the whole adult population were out skating upon it all day, and by the light of great bonfires at night. That, I think, has not happened since—nor anything approaching it.

These were indeed the champagne days—these long enchanted days on the Esk, the Wauchope and the Ewes—and the thought of them today remains as intoxicating as they must have been in actual fact all those years ago. I have been 'mad about Scotland' ever since.

There were scores upon scores of animals and birds I knew far better than I now know the domestic cat, which is the only specimen of the 'lower animals' of which I see much. My eyes may, perhaps, still seek out and recognise and appreciate a dozen or so wild flowers in the course of a year, but my memory recalls—with a freshness and a fullness of detail with which such living specimens cannot vie at all—hundreds I have not seen for over 30 years. My poetry is full of these memories: of a clump of mimulus 'shining like a dog's eyes with all the world a bone'; of the quick changes in the Esk that in a little stretch would far outrun all the divers thoughts of man since time began; of the way in which, as boys, with bits of looking-glass, we used to make the sun jump round about us. Above all, when I think of my boyhood, my chief impression is of the amazing wealth of colour. A love of colour has been one of the most salient characteristics of Scots poetry down to the best work of our contemporary poets, and I have celebrated it again and again in my own work.

Many great baskets of blaeberries I gathered on the hills round Langholm. Then there were the little hard black cranberries, and—less easy to gather since they grow in swampy places—the speckled craneberries, but above all, in the Langfall and other woods in the extensive policies of the Duke of Buccleuch, there were great stretches of wild raspberry, the fruit of which the public were allowed to pick, and many a splendid 'boiling of jam' I gathered there—gathering more than the raw material of jam, too.

I would come cycling back into Langholm down the Wauchope road with a pillowslipful of crab-apples (as at other times a basket of plovers' eggs) on my carrier; and again there was the Scrog Nut wood, shaking its bunches of nuts like clenched fists in the windy sunlight. I have nowhere seen loveliness so intense and so diverse crowded into so small a place. Langholm presents the manifold and multiform grandeur and delight of Scotland in miniature—as if quickened and thrown into high relief by the proximity of England.

There is a place at Langholm called the Curly Snake where a winding path coils up through a copse till it reaches the level whence, after passing through a field or two, it runs into the splendid woods of the Langfall. It has always haunted my imagination and has probably constituted itself as the ground-plan of my mind, just as the place called the Nook of the Night Paths in Gribo-Shov, the great forest north of Hillerod, haunted Kierkegaard's.

My boyhood was an incredibly happy one. Langholm was indeed—and presumably still is—a wonderful place to be a boy in. Scotland is not generally regarded as a land flowing with milk and honey. Nevertheless, it can do so more frequently than is commonly understood. It certainly did so in my boyhood—with a bountifulness so inexhaustible that it has supplied all my subsequent poetry with a tremendous wealth of sensuous satisfaction, a teeming gratitude of reminiscence. I still have an immense reservoir to draw upon. My earliest impressions are of an almost tropical luxuriance of nature—of great forests, of honey-scented heather hills, and moorlands infinitely rich in little-appreciated beauties of flowering, of animal and insect life, of subtle relationships of water and light, and of a multitude of rivers, each with its distinct music.

# 13

## Growing Up in the West

### by William McIlvanney

I am not without credentials. I knew the rules for playing 'Mississippi 1 2 3' before I could spell it. I still toss a tolerable milk-top. I've played 15-or-so-aside football in the muddy lee of Peeweep Hill (before the bulldozers dismantled it), heard two newcomers allotted sides by the expedient of being named 'a cock or a hen', and run through alternate lathers of sweat and shivers of coolness until the ball disappeared in dusk or a player walked off wearing one of the goalposts. While someone relayed the latest dirty story like a bulletin from the adult world, I've crouched in the long grass among my 14-year-old contemporaries, and laughed when I didn't see the joke. I have the recipe for home-brewing 'sugarally watter' below the bed. I know Glasgow on Fair Friday when drunk men have been known to address the world just after mid-day, with one arm round a companionable lamp-post. I've been on a mystery tour that ended up at Largs, seen service on the fronts of Troon, Prestwick and Ayr, where I clumsily chatted up unsuspecting girls, been waterlogged in a tent in Skye, and been a seasonal sophisticate in Arran where I danced with my girlfriend into the early hours, suave in shirt, shorts, woolly socks and sand-shoes. I've fished for meenies and beardies with an old bleach bottle, walked whuppets, sung 'Skibbereen' at Hogmanay, listened to the chaff at the bookie's corner, had friends called Rab and Jimmock and Shug. I know what a brooshie is. I think broth is always better the second day but I don't like my chips back-het. I call a spade a shovel, the mantelpiece 'the brace', the fire-grate 'the ribs', 'an acquaintance' a friend. And I don't like policemen.

In other words, I served my adolescence and graduated to

what I take for manhood in the working class of the West of
Scotland. I should imagine youth is pretty much a common
currency in most places. But it is perhaps not too fanciful to
suppose that special contour lines of experience invisibly demar-
cate certain regions from others or that the West of Scotland,
where nature and industry contend along the seaboard, is one
such region. Certainly, the towns there have always seemed to
me to form a loose fraternity, to sport flora of matching colours
and breed fauna of like habits.

My town is Kilmarnock. The population is given as around
50,000, which surprises me, since I always felt I knew most of
them. I don't know what such guide-books as there may be of
the town and district would say, but I'm fairly sure they
wouldn't mention very many of the places that have mattered
to me: The Twelve Steps, Nailer's Close, The Swinging Bridge,
Moses' Well, Mason's Ragstore—names that make up a private
mythology of childhood. It is obviously impossible in the rather
stilted perspective of adult remembrance to translate that private
experience into accessible terms without stylising the truth. So
it might be as well to formalise my memory completely and
quote from a poem I wrote a long time ago when I was trying to
crystallise for myself what my environment had meant to me:

I had the run of the day in the cobbled town,
Was cock of the leafy walk and the drayman's yard,
While the steeples kept my green and casual time
And the lazy hours drifted like thistledown
Past the square and the pub and the darkened arch
Where the coopers hammered manhood into rhyme.

I was fish to the water and fowl to the banking air,
League-booted lord of a land where in castled mills
Men wove out the sullen patterns of their mood,
Was prince of the storied dust and the sun-laid streets
Where women impassive in massive womanhood
Were folded like Sphinxes on their windowsills.

I galloped my heart's green length on the harnessed
hills.

169

Ran with the kiting clouds, with the wind was one,
Foundered in sounding grass where the breakers broke,
Barrelled my metal finger and murdered the sun,
Died at a dreaming wish and was born again,
Slept long and was safe in my woman-wanted self,
Dreaming a man till my waking, but always woke

Alone in the world with the mourning wind.

And all of the brewing and baking and shoemaking
town
With the evening shawled on its shoulders and wearing
cloud
Was calling my truant manhood to come down
Where the pubs burst with laughter, windows were
lit and loud

And the men had come home from the day with the
wagging dogs
Bundles of barking chained to their iron heels.

I followed that voice through the streets and the
omened mills

Past the curtained cat and the woman chopping logs
And before me went the pied and piping town
Playing my shadow on walls and the arable park
That cropped with couples in summer love and prams,
Singing my body up and my boyhood down
And under the private hill of an early dark.

One prosaic emendation: poetic licence apart, it would be
more accurate to call Kilmarnock the 'distilling town', since
Johnnie Walker produces whisky. The chasers are imported.
The rest can stand, I think, at least as an attempt to relate my
environment to my subsequent attempts at writing, with particular reference to two basic attitudes. The first relates to the
conflict implied here between town and country. Built above
the Barren Red Coal Measures, Kilmarnock is very much an
industrial town, but one under siege from what Pound calls 'the

green world'. The numerous parks and trees and green spaces are a strong fifth-column, and, no matter where you may stand in the town, it isn't far, as a boy runs, to the fields. For me as a boy, the country was an escape route, a place for divesting the identities the town imposed on me and going naked in my imagination. And I tend to feel that this tug-o'-war between self and community helped to determine the direction I would take when I came to try to write. I was as a boy fairly self-indulgently sensitive, given to licking near misses as well as wounds. In another context this could have made me a tyro anchorite. As it was, I became for a while passively self-absorbed. I think it is partly due to the fact that I found myself in a fairly large industrial town, where the social pressures were strong, that this self-absorption was opposed by the need to be involved a lot with other people. Both pressures have remained to offset each other and I imagine they will inform anything I try to write. Certainly, it seems to me that *Remedy is none* and *A Gift from Nessus* are both books which are essentially concerned with an individual's need to be himself and to make that self meaningful through other people. For me self-fulfilment in isolation is meaningless; you are what you are in relation to the society you live in. The second attitude is cognate with the first. It lies in the belief that writing is a social action, a way not of escaping from, but of involving yourself more deeply with other people. *Ars gratia artis* has always seemed to me a con man's slogan, about as meaningful as 'whiter than white', one worthy of MGM. How often has that Thespian lion growled on cue, to be followed by a plot in which the characters pursue their lives with the intensity of animated dollar signs? This rejection isn't very important in itself but it has more important corollaries: for example, that experimentation which is undertaken coolly and deliberately produces only novelty, whereas originality is always the result of a compulsive commitment to a truth outside the work itself.

Yet to relate these attitudes too strongly to Kilmarnock, as if I had found them growing there, is at least an over-simplification and perhaps a delusion. All I would say is that the mental climate in the West of Scotland is not conducive to the more delicate aesthetic pretensions, and Kilmarnock is typical of the West of Scotland.

But the heart of any place is the relationships you have there. Geography is people. Where I come from is my family. And I'm not sure that my family is typical of anything so much as my family. By the time I was born we were living in a council house. We seemed comfortable enough; the amenities were fine; hardship I never knew about. I don't know when it was I began to understand more about who we were: the carcasses of small perceptions silt up in you until sometimes they make an atoll, and you can see for quite a distance. Mainly, I suppose, it was a matter of seeing my mother and father in depth. It was a matter of noticing, often quite casually, over the edge of my preoccupations, how competent my mother was at being a person, which isn't such a common skill. She defused trouble of every kind, physical, emotional, financial, with calm persistence. Once I understood how comparatively poor we had always been, I wondered where she had learned the magic that alchemised a few quid into comfort. She grew with my awareness, as did my father. He was one of a diminishing working-class species—a man educated below his ability. Big words were a symptom: they frequently evaded him or metamorphosed strangely in his mouth, but his intensity was a kind of eloquent sub-language. And he wasn't averse to inventing a word where he couldn't find one. ('Snarl' is still a family adjective to describe rough weather.) He was a Fowler unto himself. More than anything else, he was himself, a separate person. From early on I was conscious of the fact that this was someone who still had his own life to live, an equation in which not all the quantities were known, that was still to be solved. Together my mother and father, my sister, my two brothers and myself made up a home that was happy without being too cosy. Too many strange winds blew in from too many quarters. Religion, politics, right and wrong, the past and the future—the arguments (they were never discussions) went on interminably, usually into the early hours of the morning, and frequently even when the facts were unable to attend.

Through it all I had a growing sense of how the stability and the comfort and the opportunities which I had taken for granted had been earned, and only with a lot of tenacity. I had a growing sense of the past. And that sense set up in me a series of dialogues which don't show much sign of abating. There were

172

plenty of voices present to start it going. Apart from having a lot of relatives, my mother and father had lived most of their lives in High Street, one of the oldest streets of the town, in one of a long line of tenements. From there they brought with them a kind of kibbutz mentality. People helped one another with flittings, sat with one another in times of illness, sought one another's advice in anything from filling up a form to treating a sick dog, and visited without warning. You knew you were having people when they came in the door—endlessly, I sometimes felt. Friends they hadn't seen for years seemed to be dropping in every other month. Uncles came mellow from the pub, cousins callow with first boyfriends. And they talked. And then talked some more.

Especially with the older people, the anecdotes threaded each other subtly until some nights were a Bayeux tapestry of stories : characters caught in characteristic poses, events picked out in luminous colours. The stories were multiform : about the six-foot-or-so Peeping Tom, an Irish labourer from the nearby lodging-house, whom my father's five feet four, wrought by contempt into a lethal weapon, reduced to bloody unconsciousness in roughly 30 seconds; about the street-sweeper who was seen in the early hours of a wet morning, walking the deserted street, under his arm a basket from which he was sowing pieces of cut paper on the cobblestones that were due to be swept next day by a colleague; about the 'daddlum-drinker' who, sitting by the bed on which his brother's life was ebbing, was stealing mouthfuls of the meths used to rub the dying man's bedsores. They were funny, sad, gruesome, grotesque, and sometimes all of these at once. They were a history, a revelation, oral scriptures.

Occurring against them, my own life had undertones of heresy, of almost sybaritic ease : a canter through secondary school, four comparatively enjoyable years at university, a degree, teaching, and a comfortable berth on the slow boat of middle-class conformity : destination—apathy. What sustained me on a course that sometimes seemed to me anathema was, first of all, my family's faith in what I was doing, and, secondly, a faith that became my own, that what I was doing was a meaningful extension of what had gone before me, and need not finish by being a sell-out. I began to think I could see a marriage between my present and the past which had been mine before I was born, and that my future could be their legitimate offspring.

That such a marriage isn't always harmonious for a working-class graduate should, I think, be obvious. A lot has been said about the problems of the working-class boy thrust by his intelligence into an academic context. But, as far as I'm concerned, the case is usually stated back to front. Much is made of the bright student forging ahead into a new life, while his alienated relatives plod the old ways, bemused and often hurt. And I've seen enough examples of something like that to understand how the myth comes about. Indeed, I've seen so many examples that I've come to believe in a kind of intellectual *nouveau riche*, those who employ their new-found intellectualism to bolster the self-containment of their own lives and to cut their families off, as it were, without any serious attempt to re-interpret the old life in terms of the new. The worst simply replace the old prejudices with the new, like taking over another man's wardrobe, and are glad to become strangers to their past; the best are painfully embarrassed by where they come from. (Or perhaps these two categories should be reversed—there certainly isn't much to choose between them.) Anyway, the saddest thing is that the families of such bright ones are frequently masochistically delighted by their 'progress'. More than once I've heard working-class parents talk with pride about a son or a daughter who is 'away above us noo'.

My own situation was hardly like that. In the first place, it has always been uncommonly hard, not to say unhealthy, for me to harbour any illusions about superior intelligence in relation to the other members of my family. Any argument would disprove them. Secondly, in the confrontation which I refereed between working-class life and university life, the latter suffered excessive punishment. In other words, my problem lay in trying to validate the new life; the old stubbornly refused to be invalidated. The new gave me the opportunity to listen to people who were prepared to speak for an hour by the clock without once involving themselves in what they were saying; urged me to consider problems the frivolous irrelevance of which was breathtaking; provided a kind of hothouse in which there could be cultivated what was to me a quite new species of dignified nonsense; and offered, it seemed to me, a way out of genuine commitment. Although it obviously contained as many follies in different guises, the old struck me as being characterised by people whose articulacy was usually inadequate in the service of their urgency, for whom problems were what you lived through, and whose commitment was a matter of survival.

Memory, of course, as well as blurring the distinctive edges, can make them too hard. But certainly the elements of past and present between which I had to arrange a marriage looked to me as incompatible as that. A few things helped to effect a *rapprochement*: there were in the English Department at Glasgow University a few lecturers who managed to relate the study of literature to what were for me real issues. Their example taught me the value of intellectuality as a means of trying to face my life more squarely, and showed me that it didn't have to be a means of opting out of it. Also, a group of us in the English class used to meet daily in the Union or the Class Library. A number of them were in the same state of dichotomy as myself. Our sessions were a sort of communal brainstorm: voices raged, the cairns of ash and cigarette stubs mounted in the ashtrays, the spilled coffee had cooled to a permanent fixture before we left, and every conversation was littered with the corpses of abandoned prejudices. I used to come out of the Union so confused about who I was supposed to be that if I'd looked in a mirror I wouldn't have been surprised to find no reflection there. Finally, this growing ability to examine the terms of my life related to the need for understanding the context from which I had come by means of a frame of reference outside itself.

Basically now my reactions to that past were twofold: admiration, for people like my parents who had survived whole in conditions of astonishing injustice; and a sense of wanton wastage, of the lives of so many others whom poverty, exploitation and social indifference had destroyed. I felt a need at least to understand that wastage, and if possible to see what had been or could be salvaged from it. My father's situation may illustrate what I mean. In a poem I have written about him I suggest that the General Strike of 1926 was for him what Midian was for Moses. He was a miner at the time and the pain of that cataclysmic event never fully left him:

> You didn't interrupt his anger when
> He brought up gouts of dead blood in his talk.

175

'Sam Harris hanged himself.' 'I've seen a wean
Whose staple diet was a dummy tit.'
'The batoned bastards beat up unarmed men,'
Not an economist's view. He didn't find
The key that locks pain safely in a law.
Raw facts still looted comfort from his mind.

It was a happening he kept going back to. I think this was
because it contained the baffling residue of all his experience,
the small recalcitrant nugget which he couldn't break down into
viable currency. Certainly, it wasn't until my own experience
had enlarged a bit that I felt capable of setting my own against
his, and came to the conclusion that they helped to interpret
each other. What I think he felt was what I feel: simply that the
most appalling thing in the world is not the vanity of human
wishes, but the vanity of human suffering; that people can endure such things as should make the world stop turning and it
may not even make their neighbours pay attention. I think it
was my reaction to that realisation as much as anything which
gave me such identity as I have, as a person and as a writer. I
believe the only worthwhile thing that can be salvaged out of
the frequently unnecessary suffering which people have gone
through, and still go through, isn't glory or admiration, or even
regret, but the bettering of the lives that come after them. And
I believe that this is only achieved through honesty, this in turn
bringing in two related skills which we don't seem too eager to
practise: the ability to admit the depth of our involvement in
the lives of others, and the ability at the same moment to allow
them room to be themselves. I take social responsibility to
mean, not the need to make sure that people keep their places,
but the need to care that each one has the right to the conditions
which will give him the chance to fulfil himself. This is to me
not primarily a political need, but simply a human one. It is
essentially a matter of the stance you adopt towards any other
person. It is at its most fundamental merely a way of seeing
other people. Probably the best illustration I can get is again a
poem, this time about my grandmother, that word which for all
of us tends to represent not so much a person as an institution:

By the time I knew my grandmother she was dead.
Before that she was where I thought she stood,

176

Spectacles, slippers, venerable head,
A standard-issue twinkle in her eyes—
Familiar stage-props of grandmotherhood.
It took her death to teach me they were lies.

My sixteen-year-old knowingness was shocked
To hear her family narrate her past
In quiet nostalgic chorus. (As they talked
Her body stiffened on the muted, fast,
Though well-washed linen coverlet of her bed.)
The kitchen where we sat, a room I knew,
Took on a strangeness with each word they said.
How she was born where wealth was pennies, grew
Into a woman before she was a girl,
From dirt and pain constructed happiness,
Shed youth's dreams in the fierce sweat of a mill,
Married and mothered in her sixteenth year,
Fed children from her own mouth's emptiness
In an attic rats owned half of, liked her beer.
Careless, they scattered pictures: mother, wife,
Strikes lived through, hard concessions bought and
    sold
In a level-headed bargaining with life.
Told anecdotes in which her strength rang gold,
Her eyes were clear, her wants as plain as salt.
The past became a mint from which they struck
Small change till that room glittered like a vault.
The corpse in the other room became to me
Awesome as Pharaoh now, as if one look
Would show me all that I had failed to see.

The kitchen became museum in my sight
Sacred as church. These were the very chairs
In which her gnarled dignity grew frail.
Her hard-won pride had kept these brasses bright.
Her tireless errands were etched upon the stairs.
A vase shone in the sun, holy as grail.
I wanted to bring others to this room,
Say it's nothing else than this that people mean,
A place to which humility can come,

A wrested niche where no one else has been
Won from the wastes of broken worlds and worse.
Here we can stay. Stupid and false, of course.
Themselves to the living is all we have to give.

My regret may be diminished but my hate
Has only grown for that in us which will
Admit each other in ourselves too late.
To fail to know another is to kill
Ourselves by subtle proxy. When will we
Have wisdom to accept the dignity
Of being just each other? Let this be
To her for wreath, gift, true apology.

Whether that poem is any good or not, I think the perception
that fostered it was a small victory in a big war. The war goes
on. It's a civil one, and in it one of my enemies is myself, the
parts of me that are constantly capitulating to sloth, indifference,
dishonesty, so that they need endlessly to be won back. It's my
sense of having allies that gives me my identity, and I don't
consider them restricted to Ayrshire or Scotland. The dishonesty
I'm talking about isn't a national monopoly, nor is the will to
combat it. The ghettos are everywhere, and they're not all made
of stone.

# 14

## Scottish Schoolmasters

### by Charles McAra

Anyone seeing this book who did not know Hector MacIver might reasonably ask: 'Who was Hector MacIver? Did he write anything? Was he a Scots poet or novelist or what?' The answer is that he was none of these things; he left behind no body of published work by which he might be remembered. What, then, did he do? He was a schoolmaster. Or to be more specific, a Scottish schoolmaster. And what vision, I wonder, does that evoke in the Home Counties or in NW1? A grim amalgam compounded in equal parts of chalk and Calvinism, or some pawky dominie from Tannochbrae, half-Doric, half-dotty?

By contrast, the English schoolmaster is well-known—indeed over-exposed—in the fiction and memoirs of the English writers who were educated at English public schools. At one time it seemed to me—wrongly, of course, I now realise—that in the Twenties and Thirties all the fashionable writers, all the worthwhile poets and novelists, were products of English public schools. And by all accounts pretty dismal places they were.

There was Greene at Berkhamstead and hell lying about him on his school desk. Sitwell scornful of Eton and Orwell miserable at the same place. And the whole thing summed up by MacNeice when he wrote:

The public schools of England have been written down *ad nauseam* . . . A young master comes up fresh from Oxford or Cambridge, full of ideas and charm; after a few years the ideas shrivel away, the charm becomes a convention . . . There were 50 masters at Marlborough, half of whom were insignificant, pleasant enough but incurably trivial, fawning on their seniors, saving up money for a sports car, backbiting each other in the Common Room. Of those who were academically brilliant the majority had stuck at a point. And the great athletes were getting stiff in the bones and short in the wind, still changed into flannels, exposed their thinning hair to the weather, but their souls lingered in ancient Wisden's Almanacs, in framed and crested photos of forgotten teams.

And so on. Yet another jaundiced report, and one that tells as much about MacNeice as about Marlborough. How, for example, does a schoolboy *know* about the backbiting in the Common Room?

But there he is, anyway, the poor English schoolmaster, an ever-fixed mark for every querulous bark. Coarse-grained and sadistic as Wackford Squeers or gentle and impotent, but undefeated as Andrew Crocker-Harris, he is familiar enough in fiction if not in fact. All this applies only to the schoolmasters at Greyfriars. It has nothing to do with schoolteachers, certificated products of training colleges and redbrick, members of the NUT, the underpaid Stakhanovites of the state system who man the secondary moderns and the comprehensives. Possibly indeed at this moment the heirs of Sillitoe and Waterhouse are observing them clinically and in the Seventies we may be in for a spate of savage recall.

But what about the Scottish schoolmaster? He is different from the English schoolmaster because Scottish education is different from English, just as Scots Law is different from English Law. In the past it has been held that 'different' meant 'superior', but I'm afraid this is no longer true. What is true is that while in England only a minority of schoolchildren are sent to public schools, in Scotland this minority is relatively much smaller. There are, I suppose, at this moment no more than about 2,000 boys being educated north of the Border in schools modelled on English lines: 19th-century innovations largely staffed by graduates of Oxbridge and grooming their abler scholars for places at particular colleges at Cambridge or Oxford. These schools, some half-dozen, have high academic standing and an enviable tradition of athletic prowess, but they are alien to the vernacular tradition.

You might visit many staffrooms in Scottish schools before you met a master who had been educated at a Scottish public school. The typical Scottish schoolmaster will have been educated at a Scottish day school, one of the local high schools or grammar schools or academies which have flourished for two or three centuries. In addition to being a graduate of a Scottish university he will have taken a year's training at a training college and not have come, like MacNeice's young master, fresh from Oxford. In short, he is an educated man, professionally well-qualified. What has happened to the notion of a Calvinist in a mortar-board enforcing discipline with the tawse and the Ten Commandments? Actually the notion is not so far-fetched, and has some foundation in the historical pressures which shaped Scottish education.

No schoolmaster anywhere is a free agent. There is always someone to whom he must answer, some authority which can appoint or dismiss him—the governors, the managers, the trustees, the education committee of the local town council. And in Scotland, roughly from the days of Knox to the time of Nelson, he was accountable to the Kirk Session or the superior court of the Kirk, the Presbytery. The popular tradition of democratic education in Scotland dates back to the mid-16th century, to the *First Book of Discipline* of the Reformers, and the tradition (or pious hope) was that in each parish there should be a schoolhouse and a schoolmaster, and in the towns and cities a high school or grammar school. The supervision of these schools was vested in the hands of the Kirk Session. They appointed the master and paid his salary. They took a lease of property and paid the rent; they reserved the right to dismiss the master if he did not perform his duties to their satisfaction; they decided the fees, however small, paid by the parents; they inspected the work of the school and saw if the pupils were progressing satisfactorily.

It is thus obvious that not only the professional ability but the whole way of life of a Scottish schoolmaster in the 17th and 18th centuries was open to the 'trial, judgment and censure' of a Kirk Session or Presbytery. It was laid down by Act of Parliament that the schoolmaster subscribe to the Westminster Confession of Faith and take an oath of allegiance to the Crown. Clearly, unless a schoolmaster was sober, diligent and faithful according to the strict interpretations of the Kirk, he was liable to find himself without a job.

These conditions no longer apply, but two lingering effects can be observed. One is that some Scottish schoolmasters are occupationally prone to turn into auld wives, prissy, precise, prim-mouthed wee men always keeking over one shoulder in case 'they' are watching. The other effect has been the direct opposite. Just as Burns was irked by the censures of the Holy Willies, so some Scottish schoolmasters have chafed against the yoke of obligatory rectitude and in a predominantly hodden grey profession have chosen to go figuratively clad in crammasy —much to the delight of pupils, who always welcome the kenspeckle, provided it is worn as a panache for proficiency and not a cloak for incompetence.

A corollary to the tradition that in each parish there should be a schoolhouse and in each town a high school was the belief that a boy of talent, however humble his circumstances, should be encouraged to make his way to one of the Scottish universities. It was probably this aspect of Scottish education that made it seem in some respects superior to the English. And although it possibly gives more prominence to the ideal dominie and the legendary 'lad o' pairts' than to the ill-paid village teacher trying to impress the three R's on some reluctant rustic hobbledehoys, it is an honourable tradition. And it is part of that tradition that the parish schoolmaster, the dominie, was a person of some local importance, esteemed for his learning and his ability to impart it.

Consider, for example, the vivid description given by Hugh Miller of parish education in the far north-east of Scotland about 1812. The grammar school at Cromarty was attended by 120 boys and some 30 girls. The building was 'a low, long, strawthatched cottage, open from gable to gable, with a mud floor below, and an unlathed roof above'. In addition to the schoolchildren, the schoolmaster had three other groups of students: young seamen who stayed ashore during the winter to study the theory of navigation; some lads anxious to learn gauging to qualify as excisemen; and grown young men who had decided to enter the Church. Two things stand out: the desire for learning and the dominie's versatility.

Other writers have left tributes to the masters of the high schools. George Borrow spent some time at the Royal High School of Edinburgh and in *Lavengro* he writes: 'well do I remember how we of the third class sat hushed and still, until the door opened, and in walked that model of a good Scotchman, the shrewd, intelligent, but warm-hearted and kind dominie, the respectable Carson.' And although Lord Cockburn, who was at the same school, recalls with some anguish the floggings he received from other masters, he speaks affectionately of the famous Rector, Dr Adam, who, he says, 'was born to teach Latin, some Greek and all virtue . . . inspiring to the boys, especially the timid and the backward; enthusiastically delighted with every appearance of talent or goodness; a warm encourager by praise, play and kindness; and constantly under the strongest sense of duty'.

The last century, of course, has seen great changes. It has seen the emergence in Scotland and England of two similar but far from identical national systems of efficient public education, concerned at first with ensuring that the newly franchised electorate was literate and today offering as one of the social services free schooling to the children of all citizens. This enormous task requires immense planning and a vast administrative superstructure composed of a government department responsible to a Minister, an inspectorate, external examining boards, local education committees. It is ponderously efficient, but it is a labyrinth in which the dominie lost his way many years ago, though every now and then you may still come across one.

Certainly when I was at school in the Thirties I was lucky enough to meet one. My English master in my last three years at school was Mr Auchterlonie, and he was the first teacher who permitted our class to enter the world of adult irony. In a dry tone he made statements—very orthodox, very proper in sentiment—which we knew to be the opposite of what he meant and we were flattered that he did not explain the joke to us. He occasionally indulged in a cynicism directed at public men and cheering crowds but he was never sarcastic at our expense, and for both these habits we were grateful. He was also very good at his job. Our pabulum in those days was a wholesome diet of Chaucer, Milton, Dryden, Pope, Addison and Steele, Coleridge and Wordsworth, Shelley and Keats, Tennyson and Browning. Modern poetry was *Reynard the Fox* by Masefield. It was greatly to his credit that he roused our interest and made this

183

fare, so costive with carbohydrates, seem palatable and even admirable. We were well-grounded, too, in such exercises as scansion and general analysis, but we were ignorant of any critical standards and unschooled in appreciation and discrimination. Since it was a Scottish school, we read Burns, of course— that is, we read 'The Cotter's Saturday Night' and *Tam o' Shanter*, but had never heard of Henryson or Dunbar or Robert Fergusson or Hugh MacDiarmid. Scots prose meant the novels of Scott: not, curiously enough, the Scotch tales, but the English ones—*Kenilworth* and *Ivanhoe*. Somehow in spite of these academic blinkers I caught a glimpse of the early poems of T. S. Eliot and when Faber published his Collected Poems in 1936 I got a first edition.

'H'm,' said Mr Auchterlonie, 'an interesting critic but a dangerous guide.'

It was intended to be discouraging. Schoolboys should not really be concerning themselves with such *dangerous* fellows as Eliot. And yet, to be fair, he lent me his copy of Huxley's *Eyeless in Gaza*, which came out about the same time.

I have recalled this to show that in Edinburgh in the late Thirties it was possible for a boy to arrive at the university eager to study literature, but woefully ill-prepared, appallingly ignorant of contemporary literature in general and in particular unaware of what was going on in his own country. Undergraduates of my acquaintance were more likely to have heard of Annie S. Swan than of Neil Gunn.

My main reason, however, in recalling the state of English teaching in the Thirties is to point the contrast that I found a decade later when, after the Second World War, I entered the English Department of the Royal High School under Hector MacIver. The chief point of contrast was one of assumptions. It was assumed from the outset that there was a living tradition of literature, that literature was not something safely dead but alive and active, possibly dangerous, liable to detonate and shatter well-cherished illusions. It was also assumed that it was possible, even in a school, to have critical standards which allowed one to reject as second-rate the work of certain writers, however 'eminent' they were supposed to be by the 'authorities'. Above all, it was assumed that it was possible to detect the arrival of a new poet of talent *before* he had received the accolade of a Foyle's Lunch, the Queen's Medal or the Associate Professorship in Creative Communication at Dick Van Dyke University.

Hector MacIver became one of the outstanding teachers of English in Scotland in the two decades immediately after the war. This may sound like a very large claim, but its truth can be supported in three ways: by the achievements of his best pupils; by the intellectual stimulus and pleasure he gave to hundreds of boys who had no pretensions as English specialists; and by the way in which through his own example and enthusiasm he taught a large number of young English masters their job and encouraged them to go on to posts of higher responsibility.

He was himself a product of the school of Grierson, under whom he studied at Edinburgh University in the early Thirties and with whom he stayed for a number of years. And with Sir Herbert he shared a deep admiration for Donne and the Metaphysical poets, for Sir Walter Scott and for the prose of the Authorised Version of the Bible. In addition there was his own predilection for the Border Ballads and the poetry of Yeats. His knowledge of literature, of the theatre, of the art of writing, was enriched by his activities outside the school walls. An accomplished radio broadcaster and actor in Gaelic and English, he contributed more than a hundred talks, reviews, plays to the Scottish Home Service from 1935 onwards.

In the classroom he did two things superlatively well. The first was to communicate to boys the idea that, with a little effort, they could enter into a poem and gain a foothold on the poet's creative imagination. Poems that seemed at first sight difficult or obscure made sense, and pupils who had, perhaps a little timidly, entered the round Zion of the water bead and the synagogue of the ear of corn were soon on their 18th year to heaven or Downing College. The other thing he did was to insist that the prose boys wrote themselves should be fresh and imaginative, lucid, precise and accurate. Though no man taught less for results—in the sense of flogging the dead horses of Eng Lit because they 'come up' in exams—yet the results came and his many years of successful and adventurous teaching were recognised by the award of an adult scholarship to Balliol to do research on sixth-form studies.

MEMOIRS OF A MODERN SCOTLAND

It would be wrong, however, to give the impression that he was some plaster paragon. He had his own private scale of priorities in such mundane matters as mark-sheets, report-cards and registers. Like most Western Islanders he had evolved an efficient technique for coping with the importunities of the clock-ridden inhabitants of the Central Lowlands. He had his own particular brand of protective elusiveness and all the Gael's propensity for benign procrastination. And in his make-up there was more than a hint of crammasy.

In print the best way, perhaps, to convey this colourfulness of character is not by anecdote but by analogy. He was like some of the individuals he admired. Let me name no more than three. There was James Crichton of Eliock, the Admirable Crichton, scholar, linguist, swordsman, challenging all-comers in disputation or fencing at Paris, Genoa, Venice. There was James Graham, the Great Marquis, combing his long hair in the Tolbooth before his execution and, when reproved, answering: 'My hair is still my own. Tonight, when it will be yours, treat it as you please.' And going out to the scaffold at the Mercat Cross as if to a wedding, wearing his richly laced scarlet cloak, his carnation silk stockings, ribbons on his shoes, white gloves on his hands. And there was the other Graham, Don Roberto, most aristocratic of radicals, arriving at Trafalgar Square on that Bloody Sunday in the 1880s and nonchalantly making his way with John Burns through the ranks of mounted police, relying on sheer effrontery and a gentle touch with horses, and only just failing to reach Nelson's Column before being clobbered by the police. The common factors are guts, moral courage, audacity, a liking for the bold stroke or the *beau geste*. These were the qualities MacIver esteemed and displayed in his own life and from them came the colour, a kind of impudent gaiety which defeats 'all the rest, sullen anger, solemn virtue, calculating anxiety, gloomy suspicion, prevaricating hope'.

Since he was a Lewisman and native to the sea and small ships it was inevitable that during the war he should choose to serve in the small ships of the Royal Navy—in destroyers and as the First Lieutenant of an escort vessel. It was an experience that left a mark on his personality as indelible as a killick tattooed on a matelot's arm. It sharpened the aplomb and audacity which were essential features of his personality. Hector MacIver never forgot the Navy. It showed in his saltier idioms and in his respect for the customs of the service. It showed in other ways, too. There is a type of Scottish Nationalist, girning and thrawn, downing his dram to the neurotic toast: 'Here's tae us. Wha's like us? Damn few an' they're a' deid!' MacIver was a Scot and by instinct and temperament a Scottish Nationalist as perfervid as the Arbroath Declaration, but he did not suffer from creeping Anglophobia. He supported and admired the writers of the Scottish Renaissance, but was never so deafened by the piping of the whaups on the Moorfoots that he could not hear the nightingales singing south of the Border. It was typical, perhaps, that his last 'find' was not some Abbotsford bard proclaiming that he 'wad parle nae leid but Lallans' but a Cornishman and, like himself, an ex-Navy schoolmaster, Charles Causley.

MacIver's career as a schoolmaster also illustrates another recurring feature of Scottish life—the way in which the centre is replenished from the periphery. MacDiarmid, for example, is not a native of Glasgow or Edinburgh. He comes from Langholm, which is as far south from the capital in miles and in spirit as the Border Ballads in which it figures—'Johnnie Armstrong' and 'Lord Maxwell's Goodnight'. Today, when the greater part of the population of Scotland is crammed into the gritty multi-storied concrete conurbations of the Forth-Clyde complex, life for the majority there is so mechanised, computer-based and neon-lit that the prevailing standards and aspirations are common to urban communities everywhere from Slough to Seattle. Far to the north and west, however, across the Minch or beyond the Pentland Firth, familiar with gales and long, dark winters, are the islanders. Nothing would be more misleading than to romanticise them as Tourist Board attractions, quaint fey creatures fathered by Whisky Galore on Mary Rose. All I wish to emphasise is that they are different, with a difference in their ways that can be damnably exasperating at times to a mainlander, but with a difference which also manifests itself, happily, in the particular cast of their imagination, in their sensibility and insight. When the islander is a man of talent, he is able in his art or craft to offer refreshment and vigour, a welcome sanity and wholesomeness, to the cultural life of the centre. In poetry this is true of men like Edwin Muir and George Mackay Brown. And in the more prosaic daily routine of schoolmastering it was true of Hector Mac-Iver.

# 15

# The Emergence of Scottish Music

## by Ronald Stevenson

I first met Hector MacIver one evening in a pub on Edinburgh's 'amber mile'—Rose Street. It would be some time in the Fifties. Within a few minutes of our meeting, we had got on to Scottish music and soon he was singing—I remember his pleasant baritone—songs from his native Isle of Lewis. And very unusual songs they were: no 'sangs o' the cratur' but strangely serene psalm tunes sung in the Gaelic, with no less than ten, and sometimes more than a dozen, notes to each syllable. Such long-linked melismas I had never heard in any other vocal music. They suggested a vocal 'transcription' of highly ornamented bagpipe music. They also suggested those curious involuted knot-designs of medieval Celtic carvings, brooches and crosses.

Ten years passed before I heard this kind of song again. The occasion was a public lecture given in the National Library of Scotland one summer's evening in 1967, when Dr Thorkild Knudsen, a remarkable Danish folk-musicologist, spoke on 'The Singing and Intoning of Gaelic Poetry'. He played a recording of a woman 'precenting' in a croft on Lewis, and I immediately recognised the kind of music Hector MacIver had sung. Very shortly before Dr Knudsen's lecture, the Edinburgh Festival had featured some sensational so-called *avant-garde* compositions: I couldn't help but reflect, as I sat there in the lecture audience, that the psalms from Lewis were as new as any self-consciously super-modern music. These Lewis psalms were new music all right: music of great antiquity but perennial. It had been kept alive by a great oral tradition and was quietly flourishing in the Highlands and Islands at the same time that the Scottish Renaissance was burgeoning in the Lowlands, in the Thirties. Yet hardly anybody except the singers knew anything about it.

189

With the Scottish Renaissance came a realisation of the contribution of Gaelic music to Scottish culture—a glimmering of
realisation. The composer Francis George Scott made a tentative study of it, late in his career; and Hugh MacDiarmid wrote
with vision of the Great Music of the pipes, both in his poetry and
in the author's note to his book *The Islands of Scotland*. But
even now, in the aftermath of the Scottish Renaissance, the
subject of Gaelic music, and particularly pibroch, remains unexplored by most musicians: unexplored, yet often glibly dis-
missed as of little consequence. Yet it is in Gaelic music that
Scotland finds its identity, more than in the music of the Lowlands, for Lowland song has much in common with Northum-
brian song (think only of the Tyneside tune 'The Keel Row'),
whereas Gaelic music evinces unique features. Gaelic music is
traditionally divided into two categories: *Ceòl Mór* (literally, the
Great Music) and *Ceòl Beag* (literally, the Small Music). These
correspond to 'serious' and 'light' music. *Ceòl Mór* consists ex-
clusively of the pibroch, the classical variation-form of solo
instrumental music performed on the Great Highland Bagpipe.
*Ceòl Beag* consists of vocal music (*puirt-a-beul* or mouth-music,
and songs secular and sacred) and instrumental dance music
(strathspeys, reels and jigs), marches or slow airs, for fiddle,
clarsach (Celtic harp), small dance-band, bagpipe or pipe-band.

The most salient idiosyncrasy of Gaelic music is the scale of
the Great Highland Bagpipe, which may be approximated in
notation like this:

1  2  3  4  5  6  7  8  9

The cross (+) signifies approximately
a quarter-tone sharp

This scale comprises a pentatonic structure (degrees 1, 2, 3, 5,
6, 8 and 9) plus two microtones (degrees 4 and 7), and it
offers the only instance of microtonal music indigenous to the
British Isles. Indeed, by virtue of its microtones, this scale has
more in common with Indian ragas than with any other British
music. A ratio exists between the structure of this scale and the
structure of the Gaelic language. Gaelic, as an Indo-European
language, contains a main vocabulary of European-rooted

words and a residual element of Sanskrit words. The Gaelic word *seòmar* (room) derives from the French *chambre*, and such derivation is demonstrable for most Gaelic words, many of them relating to Latin. But there are a few Gaelic words which relate directly to Sanskrit—generally words signifying basic aspects of life. For example:

| Scots Gaelic | Sanskrit |
|---|---|
| *Ann,* in existence | *An,* to exist |
| *Meidh,* a measure | *Mátra,* a measure |
| *Ceilidh,* a musical foregathering | *Khéli,* a song |
| *Mór,* great | *Mahá,* great |
| *Màrbh,* to die | *Mára,* death |

The microtones of the Great Highland Bagpipe scale are the residual 'Sanskrit' element, persisting as if in token of the trans-European trek of the Celts from their obscure Caucasian genesis.

Just how problematic the subject of pibroch can be is demonstrated by a cutting from the *Observer* which a friend recently passed on to me (it was published some time in 1967):

## Scottish Enigma

Experts have been puzzled by a new record of bagpipe music played by Pipe-Major Iain McLeod. Now it turns out that the tapes were recorded backwards. More than 1,000 records went out without anyone realising the mistake. And 400 were sold without complaint. After the sitar, could this be the next new sound?

Seriously, problems posed by the assimilation of pibroch elements into music other than for bagpipes—comparable to Bartók's assimilation of Hungarian ethno-musical elements or Szymanowski's absorption of the music of the Polish Highlands —are considerable and recalcitrant.

The MacCrimmons of Skye, hereditary pipers to the MacLeod of Dunvegan Castle for three centuries from *circa* 1620, perfected the highly stylised, complex and sophisticated variation-form of pibroch at a time when the variation-form of the Tudor virginalists was embryonic. But no non-piping composer seems to have interested himself in pibroch until Sir Alexander

Mackenzie (1847–1935), who wrote a *Pibroch Suite* for violin and orchestra, which Sarasate performed at the Leeds Festival of 1889. Mackenzie's German training is discernible in the idea of straitjacketing the flowing variation-form of pibroch into the sectionalised form of suite.

The next generation of Scottish composers, including Hamish MacCunn (1868–1916)—a sketchy composer—and Sir John Blackwood McEwen (1868–1948)—a meticulous one—are alike in that they manifest their Scottishness only by giving their work a patina of local colour. (McEwen's best contribution to Scottish music is his bequest which provides for annual concerts and triennial commissions of Scottish works at the University of Glasgow.)

A generation later, the first Scottish composer of European stature appears: Francis George Scott (1880–1958). He was composing before World War I though he is inseparably associated with the Scottish Renaissance movement and, as Hugh MacDiarmid's acknowledged mentor, was in some ways its inspirer. He was essentially an autodidact, though a few lessons from Roger Ducasse increased his sympathy for French music, which at least freed him from the old bugbear of subservience to German hegemony. It was Scott's sympathy for French music which determined his approach to attempts at absorbing pibroch influences. That is, some of his later music is imbued with an Impressionism which suggests the a-rhythmic aspect of pibroch and its impersonal ethos, which removes it from somatic emotionalism. The a-rhythmic aspect of pibroch results from the piper's *rubato* ('robbed time') tradition of performance and from the accumulative ornamentation which increases with the successive variations and which has the effect of cancelling out regularity of beat. Hugh MacDiarmid has written perceptively of this in his poem 'Lament for the Great Music', when he sings of the pibroch's being

> Deliberately cast in a non-rhythmic mould
>     because the composers knew
> That rhythm is an animal function,
>     whereas poetry and music,
> Involving no bodily activity of the artist
>     in their making,

Can exist in a purely psychological
relation to society
And would be equally 'true' in a world
of disembodied spirits.

From a total of 99 solo songs, published from 1922 to 1949, there are eight which evince Scott's awareness of pibroch. In the Burns setting 'Mary Morison' (1922), Scott's questioning attitude towards traditional rhythm is demonstrated when he instructs in a footnote that the triple pulse-rhythm is to be felt not as the traditional — ᴗ ᴗ but as — — ᴗ and the quadruple pulse-rhythm is to be felt not as the traditional — ᴗ — ᴗ but as — — ᴗ ᴗ. His setting of MacDiarmid's 'The Eemis Stane' (1924) captures something of pibroch's 'disembodiedness' in an idiom that owes allegiance to French Impressionism, mainly through pedal-held sound in the accompaniment. The coda of another MacDiarmid setting, 'Hungry Waters' (1925), also suggests the remoteness of pibroch and hints at the bagpipe's drone and 'warbling' ornamentation. A similar remoteness permeates another MacDiarmid setting, 'The Innumerable Christ' (published 1949). Two late Scott songs—'St Brendan's Graveyard' (1931, poem by Jean Lang) and 'To a Loch Fyne Fisherman' (published 1939, poem by George Campbell Hay)—actually direct the interpretation to be 'like a pibroch, impersonal and without nuance, aloof'. The bars of the Lang setting are indicated only by dotted lines, signifying an accentless rhythm. Another MacDiarmid setting, 'Milkwort and Bog-Cotton' (1932), goes even further and is unbarred:

By permission of Bayley & Ferguson, Glasgow

All these Scott songs suggest pibroch through quantitative, 'timeless' rhythm, not through dynamic stress-accent but through agogic accent which ultimately relates to speech and its vowel-gradation (ablaut) and vowel-mutation (umlaut): that is, to the pneumatic life-act of breathing and to spiritual inspiration, not the somatic and corporeal.

But Scott never explored the melodic nature of pibroch very far. The opening of his MacDiarmid setting 'The Watergaw' (published 1939) presents a melodic structure based on the following scale:

This bears a distant relationship to the Great Highland Bagpipe scale because it adds two inflected notes (degrees 3 and 5) to a gapped mode (degrees 1, 2, 4 and 6). This relationship to pibroch was almost certainly intuitive and indicates the acuity of Scott's intuition. But intuition is not enough to coalesce pibroch and other European music.

Scott's last work, *Intuitions*, a set of miniatures for piano, contains a few attempts at piano transcription of pibroch *urlars* (that is, the initial, basic *materia musica* out of which pibroch is made). Though his *oeuvre* contains some piano music, an organ piece (1912), a few choral items and a very few orchestral scores, it is as a song composer that Scott is most representative. His range of interest was wide and set him apart from both his Scottish predecessors and contemporaries. He was aware of Schoenberg's music even in the Twenties, when Schoenberg was unknown to most British musicians. There is no other British music from the Twenties that is nearer to Schoenberg's 12-note idiom than certain passages in Scott's MacDiarmid songs: in particular 'Country Life', 'Crowdieknowe' and 'Moonstruck'. His versatility enabled him to write naïve modern folk-songs and sophisticated, experimental art-songs.

Ian Whyte, who died in 1960, for many years conductor of the BBC Scottish Orchestra, sensibly worked within his limitations. In one work, the ballet *Donald of the Burthens* (Covent Garden, 1951), he rises above his many pleasant folk-song settings and orchestrations. Limiting himself to *Ceòl Beag* (the 'small' music), he wrote a finale which juxtaposes symphony orchestra, unaccompanied mouth-music and a bagpipe reel, the pipes being accompanied by the orchestra. The sudden changes of medium exhilarate like a breath of caller air.

Erik Chisholm (1904–65) wrote a *'Pibroch' Piano Concerto, 'Pibroch' Variations* for piano solo, and *'Pibroch' Dances* for orchestra, as well as many Scottish folk-song and folk-dance settings, a volume of which is published by the USSR State Publishing House. He attempted to absorb pibroch into the mainstream of European music, but the *'Pibroch' Dances* (a self-contradictory title) show a misconception of the nature of pibroch and a curious confusion of the *Ceòl Mór* with the *Ceòl Beag*. He also wrote a *'Hindu' Piano Concerto*, operas, ballets, symphonic works, chamber music and songs.

William Wordsworth (born 1908), a relative of his namesake, the poet, has composed much, including a series of five symphonies. His *Highland Overture* (1964) has a granitic quality that places it above mere 'local colour'. His *Valediction* for piano (1967) is based on the bi-modal idea of underpinning a pentatonic structure, with G as its tone-centre, by an octave pedal on E flat which clashes with the E natural in the pentatonic mode employed. This coincidentally (or intuitively, or atavistically) relates to the ancient practice of pipers tuning their drones dissonantly in order that they would sound over a greater distance in the open air than consonantly tuned drones would.

Robin Orr (born 1909) has written a *Symphony in one movement* (1963) which achieves Scottishness without using folk material. He has also written an opera, *Full Circle* (libretto by Sydney Goodsir Smith), which is set in the Glasgow slums during the depression years of the Thirties. This is the first indigenous opera to be produced by Scottish Opera (1968).

Cedric Thorpe Davie (born 1913), though he has stopped composing and considers himself an encourager of young musicians, has contributed to Scottish music by consistently composing in a Scottish idiom in his film and radio scores. His cantata *The Jolly Beggars* (poem by Burns) has enjoyed popularity through its recording by the Saltire Singers.

Iain Hamilton (born 1922) was commissioned by the Burns Federation to write a work commemorating the poet's bicentenary in 1959. The resultant *Symphony for two orchestras* displayed an interest in technical experiment without showing any Scottish attributes, either by general character (as in the Orr symphony) or by reference to traditional Scottish music. He has composed a set of *Scottish Dances* for orchestra set in a syncopated American idiom.

Encouraged by Hamilton, Thea Musgrave (born 1928) has written a *Scottish Dance Suite* for orchestra. She has also set Scottish poets, ranging from Dunbar to Maurice Lindsay, who has been her librettist for two operas, both of them Scottish in subject but composed in an idiom that avowedly owes more to Central Europe than to Scotland.

If the history of Scottish music has been obscure to Scottish composers, they now have no excuse for remaining ignorant about it because Francis Collinson's book *The Traditional and National Music of Scotland* is a comprehensive survey of the subject and contains the most detailed and accurate account of pibroch to date. Collinson is the first non-piper to write a pibroch for the Great Highland Bagpipe, *Lament for Calum MacLean*. He was a founder member of the School for Scottish Studies, Edinburgh University, which, since 1951, has engaged in folk-musicological field-work. This industry is admirable, but if the material does not act as a catalyst to new music in a distinctively Scottish idiom, as similar material did in the case of Bartók and Kodály, the School of Scottish Studies will be a cultural sarcophagus.

Dr Kenneth Elliot has also done original and much-needed research into the medieval music of Scotland and the music of the Scottish Court, some of which he has edited, performed and recorded.

In my own work as a composer (I was born in 1928 in Blackburn, Lancashire, of Scottish descent) I have set 20 MacDiarmid poems, concentrating, unlike F. G. Scott, on the later poetry. I have followed Francis Collinson's lead and, like him, a non-piper, have written a pibroch for pipes, *Calum Salum's Salute to the Seals* (1967). I have also set Gaelic poems by Sorley Mac-Lean in a choral cycle (not based on folk material). This was commissioned by the Greenock Gaelic Choir and is entitled *Anns an Airde, as an Doimhne* (1968) ('In the Heights, from the Depths'). The first song sings of nature's majesty in the Scottish

Highlands; the second is a dirge about mankind's misery in the Lowland slums; and the last song contrasts the remote beauty of the nocturnal universe and the 'only true miracle of human love'. In my *Passacaglia on DSCH* (1962), for piano, simulating the bagpipe scale by means of major/minor coalescence in place of the microtones, I have introduced the *urlar* of the 17th-century pibroch *Cumha na Cloinne* ('Lament for the Children') by Patrick Mór MacCrimmon, who composed the pibroch in memory of seven of his eight sons who died in one year. I have recast the *urlar*, thinking of the child victims of Nazism.

I have not dealt with the place of Scottish music in the Edinburgh Festival, because it doesn't have a place as yet—though the Scottish National Orchestra, the BBC Symphony Orchestra and the Edinburgh Festival Choir contribute to it.[1]

It may be coming yet that the habitués of the howfs of Edinburgh's Rose Street will blether about Scotland's music as they do now about Scottish fitba; and MacIver's croon will be echoed by others; and the rose of a nation's music will come 'loupin oot frae the camsteerie plant' of the Knoxian cantankerous thistle that Scottish music has been so far. As Sydney Goodsir Smith would say, 'mebbe.'

[1] Perhaps I need to emphasise that my subject is 'Scottish Music', not 'Music in Scotland'. Readers desiring a more generalised view might consult the Scottish Music Archive, established at the University of Glasgow in 1969. Scotland, unlike Wales, has no autonomous Guild of Composers but has a Scottish Branch of the Composers' Guild of Great Britain, founded in 1966. Though I have not dealt with musicians who have not occupied themselves with specifically Scottish music, an exception must be made in the case of Sir Donald Francis Tovey (1875–1940), who contributed notably to the awakening of musical consciousness in the capital of Edinburgh, where he occupied the chair of music at the University from 1914 till his death. Scholar, composer and pianist, in his self-assessment he was a populariser of music. His Workers Educational Association evening classes in Edinburgh enrolled the record-breaking total of 150 members.

# 16

## The Backwardness of Scottish Television

### by Stuart Hood

By what criteria can we judge the quality of a country's television? One is the range and variety of the programmes offered to the viewer. Another is the degree of freedom it enjoys to show and speak the truth. A third is its success in revealing a society to itself: on a primitive level by showing its citizens how they speak, behave, live, and on another higher level by revealing to them the mechanics of their society, how it functions politically, economically and culturally. All three criteria are linked. For it is not possible to deal in truth unless there is a sufficiently wide spectrum of programmes to include those which honestly explore the nature of society. No society can be explored unless its broadcasters are free to ask honest questions and answer them. Unless broadcasters are allowed this minimum of freedom, self-revelation is impossible. All over the world there are societies, ranging from great modern capitalist or socialist states to small, emergent, underdeveloped ones, which have not achieved self-awareness because the dominant instruments of mass culture do not provide a mirror in which their citizens can see themselves truthfully. In most countries television is now the main disseminator of mass culture. In many of them it has either failed in its duties or been prevented from performing them.

The reasons for this failure are various. Television may be in the hands of men who are more interested in its potentialities as a vending machine than as a means of communicating truth: truth which may be either fictional or documentary, there being as much truth about society or human behaviour in a good play as in a good piece of reporting. Television may be dominated by a state machine which fears that if the official explanation of

how men live, the official description of their motives and aspirations, is challenged, the whole fabric of society may be en-
dangered. In a monolithic society television can deal in no other
truths than received ones. It was, therefore, one of the most
striking indications of how far Czechoslovakia had retreated
from Stalinism when Czech television allowed its viewers to
become aware of shared emotions, shared but long-repressed
judgments on their rulers, shared aspirations, which had never
been exposed on the air. Conversely, it is one of the symptoms
of the degeneration of French democracy that French television
has for years played a subservient role to the French government
and, particularly in the field of news and current affairs, accepted
detailed government direction. 'How can one govern without
television?' André Malraux has asked. He speaks with authority.
French television hid the truth about the Algerian War and the
brutalities which were an inherent part of it; they had their aftermath in the police brutalities in the Sorbonne. It is true that by
the time the students' barricades had gone up the staff of French
television and radio had, to its honour, gone on strike; but in the
early days of the student revolt French television news had, in
line with government policy, given only a one-sided paternalistic
account of the issues underlying student unrest.

In the worst case of all are those countries too poor or too
backward to have an indigenous television service. Throughout
the world there are television stations consisting of a tiny news
studio and a minimum of ancillary equipment—resources so
meagre that with them one can transmit only pre-recorded programmes, packaged series supplied predominantly by the great
American networks. Such stations represent a type of cultural
colonialism which cannot be justified by saying that the viewers
soon become avid consumers of the manufactured dreams of
the West. The West has a long tradition in the supply of opiates.
Not that the puritanical documentaries of the East are any more
truthful—merely less entertaining. It can be argued that in these
cases television is merely moving into a cultural vacuum. All
over the world old cultures are dying. This is not necessarily
in itself tragic: cultures have no more claim to immortality than
we have ourselves. What is regrettable is that they appear to
have lost the power of propagation. There is no natural local
replacement, no autochthonous renewal. On the one hand, we

find the artefacts of ancient cultures artificially produced long after they have ceased to have any social utility or cultural significance: the ritual carvings of the hunter, the incantatory drums, the spears, the camel bridles beaded against the evil eye, are mass-produced for sale in the lobbies of the international hotels and the trinket shops of the international airports. On the other hand, old oral cultures go down before the soap opera, *The Saint, Hitchcock's Half-Hour* and the rudimentary folklore of the Wild West, which for some of the viewers may represent the West itself. If such sterile fantasies are disseminated to the cafés, bars and bazaars, and to those miserable fly-infested slums where any culture died long ago, it is because they face no opposition.

There are countries which do oppose television precisely because they have strong cultural, social and religious traditions. South Africa is one example. Narrow Protestantism has there combined with fear of exposing the African population to material produced outside the ethical boundaries laid down by apartheid and the Reformed Church to postpone the introduction of a television service. Israel, which has only recently taken its first steps in television, is another case. There resistance to the new medium, powerfully led by David Ben-Gurion, was based on a number of social and moral objections. It was argued that television must necessarily lead to the trivialisation of life—a distraction of the nation from the hard task it had set itself; that it was likely to undermine the foundations of the theocratic state of Israel by promoting secular attitudes; that it would in so doing destroy old and valuable traditions brought to the new state from Europe, from Africa and Asia; and that it would personalise politics. There was a subsidiary—and to some people more acceptable—argument that a country which, while not technically underdeveloped, is still in an economic position of some difficulty, since it must retain large armed forces and at the same time resettle the ingathered Jews from whatever quarter of the world they choose to come, has neither the financial nor the technical resources to sustain a television service. It was therefore for many years low on any list of priorities. But the Six Day War persuaded the government that there was something ridiculous in a situation where a considerable number of Jews not only owned television sets but watched programmes from the Arab countries. Television was therefore installed for two reasons. One was the calculation that, by overflowing the borders of Israel, as it must do in this tightly packed corner of the Mediterranean, it might help to counter the crasser forms of anti-Israeli propaganda. The other was the hope that it might conceivably do something else: help to further the coalescence of a nation which inevitably, because its citizens have such diverse backgrounds and such different cultural levels, contains within its borders disparate cultural groups. Television, which can speak even to the illiterate or semi-literate, may provide a link by providing a number of what may broadly be described as cultural experiences shared by Ashkenazim and Sephardim, by European and Oriental Jews alike.

Scotland does not fit easily into any of the categories discussed above. It is not in any sense of the word—unless one thinks of the neglect of the Highlands—an underdeveloped country. It does have certain cultural and moral traditions but they are part of a broken-backed culture. Its Renaissance was late and blighted. Its only claimant to the title of Renaissance prince died at Flodden. Its Gaelic culture was destroyed along with the social system that nurtured it. Its Age of Enlightenment came when the pull of London was already overwhelming: witness Robert Adam—he had financed his Grand Tour by working as Master Mason at Fort George, the northern bastion against the clans—returning from Rome to set up an architect's practice not in Edinburgh but in London. The 19th century began with sentimental Jacobitism and ended in the Kailyard. The 20th century saw Gaelic poets writing in a language fewer people spoke with each decade; other poets engaged in the fruitless attempt to keep alive the dialects of Lowland Scotland as a vehicle for serious literary work. Here, if ever, there was, when television (and before it radio) arrived, a cultural vacuum. Broadcasting moved into it and spoke to the people in the accents of the manse. The BBC was and is, by its nature, respectful of established centres of power, but its Scottish Region was notorious for its subservience to the Scottish Establishment. It bowed low to St Andrew's House, to the Kirk, to the Glasgow civic authorities, to the great Highland landowners and the great Clydeside industrialists. When the BBC in London and elsewhere was moving forward and in a spirit of responsible inquiry was encouraging its television and radio reporters to seek the truth beneath official statements, Scotland dragged behind. Television reporters in particular, on crossing the Border, found that the Scottish BBC expected them to conform to a more respectful, a less radical norm of behaviour. There was, moreover, a local censorship to which programmes on Scottish themes had to be submitted; fortunately the arrangement was not usually respected. This was an era when few programmes about or from Scotland were shown on the BBC's national network. The inquiring spirits were unwilling to put up with the petty interference with their work. Local enterprise was lacking, not because of any lack of talent, but because of lack of encouragement to be bold. It is significant that the documentary *Culloden* was conceived, produced and edited in London. What the Scottish viewers were offered, and what the national network was offered, was sentimental Scottish singing by young men in full Highland fig. The BBC failed to discharge its duty, which is to reflect the life and culture of the nation in all its diversity. But if Scotland was neglected by television the fault was to be sought in Scotland itself.

Nor did commercial television in the form of ITV, although avowedly dedicated to the concept of regionalism, do much better. Its franchises were, from the beginning, granted on a regional basis. There has always been, in the public pronouncements of the Independent Authority, considerable stress on the need for license-holders to mirror the local life of their areas. It might have been expected, therefore, that Scottish commercial television would have taken the opportunity offered by the BBC's shortcomings to develop strong regional programmes which, besides satisfying local audiences, might have been good enough to be accepted for showing throughout the rest of the independent network. But this did not happen. Instead, in the early days, STV decided to blanket the industrial belt of Scotland with entertainment which lacked roots even in the urban culture of the area. It was sad to see programmes being bought for the Scottish viewer which their American salesmen were unable to dispose of elsewhere in the United Kingdom. Grampian Television, lacking the resources or the revenue to make more than a very few programmes on its own account, could not itself redress the balance. Nor could Border Television, whose franchise covered the old 'debatable land'. Yet it was Grampian Television that produced a programme on Mary Slessor of Calabar which, although modest, was shown on the network and was an example of the kind of programme that deserved to find national acceptance.

If Scottish television is to discharge its duty to Scotland by revealing the nation to itself, it will most easily achieve its aims by developing its output of documentaries: for the documentary is not only the most important form of television journalism, it is the best weapon for critical analysis of social conditions. It has its roots in the Grierson tradition—a tradition which has, however, been radically modified since its inception. The tradition of *Drifters* began to peter out in 'well-made' documentaries which lacked the edge the present generation of film-makers require to go with their more aggressive approach. It is easy in Scotland to be seduced by pretty pictures and the kind of facile romanticism that goes with them; but that is not what Scottish television should be concerned to show. What it should bring to the screen with all their variety of accent and behaviour are the men and women who make the modern nation. Paradoxically, there is reason to believe that the more firmly a programme is anchored in local reality, the more rigorously it is directed towards exploring some local (but not parochial) problem, the more interesting it is likely to prove to a wider audience, and therefore the more likely to be accepted for showing on the national networks.

It would be untrue to say that none of the subjects that suggest themselves have been touched on: various magazine programmes have dealt with areas of Scottish life briefly and cursorily. The problem of Highland development has been dealt with in this way; but there has so far been on British television no major documentary on the social and economic plight of the Highlands. The Sunday supplements have been allowed to get in first. On an entirely different level the role of the Church in Scotland has not, outside the limits of religious broadcasts, been analysed on the screen. The General Assembly has some claim to be considered, if not a national parliament, at least a national forum. There is material there for a documentary which if well and honestly made—and the Church would require to co-operate to achieve that honesty—must be of more than merely local interest. Scottish education is still mentioned with legendary awe in the south. Does it still stand where it did when men like my father, who sat under Kelvin at Glasgow University, went out after graduation to be the headmaster of three- or four-teacher village schools? Or is it true that Scottish education has lagged behind, thorough but unadventurous, narrow in its aims as compared to the best of English education? Are the Scottish universities on as high a level as their English counterparts? What are the students like? What, if anything, distinguishes them from their contemporaries south of the Border? What do they think about Scotland?

These are themes drawn from what Marxists would call the social superstructure of Scotland. There are other programmes to be made on the country's economic life and its relationship to that of the United Kingdom. The effects of area development such as must follow in Fife and Angus from the building of the new bridges, the consequences of the Moray Firth development plan, the effects of such plans on the countryside and the life of the communities involved—all these are subjects crying out for treatment. Then there are social problems which, although general throughout the United Kingdom, have particular local manifestations: the gang warfare of Glasgow, for example, which has in the past been occasionally discussed in magazine programmes (produced in London)—and then in the teeth of local opposition from BBC officials and from civic authorities who objected to exploration of the social causes underlying the violence.

There will be difficulties in accustoming the Scottish public, which at its worst can be ineffably smug, to seeing honest inquiries into Scottish society and to co-operating in the effort to discover the truth. But even greater difficulties are likely to be found in the field of creative writing for television—and in particular in television drama. Here the concentration of talent in London is very great. There are few writers in Scotland with any reputation as writers for the medium. They are cut off from the best producers and from that flow of professional knowledge which is essential if a school of television writing is to flourish. The acting profession, too, is London-based, and the cost of importing the cast for a large-scale production is bound to inflate the already high costs of television drama. The BBC has indeed built studios in Glasgow suitable for drama production, but they have tended to be thought of as supplementing the resources available in the London production complex. The productions which have come from them have been largely adaptations, and not necessarily of books with Scottish themes. The same policy emerges in BBC serials, which, when set in Scotland, have exploited the Scottish landscape rather than Scottish life. What is required is the encouragement of a school of realist writing—the style best suited to television—which would be as true to the life and accents of Glasgow or Edinburgh as the early episodes of *Z Cars* were to Liverpool. This would call for a degree of regional courage, for realism tends to produce strong resentments: the BBC North Region's first instinct was to disown *Z Cars*. But both on a popular and on a higher creative level regional accents must be heard. Indeed it is one of the paradoxes of television that while being, on the one hand, an instrument of assimilation, it has let us hear the accents in the months of characters conceived by David Mercer and David Turner, for instance, and in the work of the London school of film-makers whose productions included *Cathy Come Home*. It is significant that such programmes have usually been radical in inspiration and execution—which may be one reason why in the past the process has stopped short at the Border. We have still to see on television a dramatic character who will express the almost Neapolitan qualities of the Glaswegian or the feel of east-windy,west-endy Edinburgh society. The enemies of realistic drama on Scottish themes will as always be sentimentalism and the fear that honest plays might give Scotland a bad name.

There have been times when those sitting at the centre of BBC Television, faced by the enormous demands of the medium and contemplating the lack of true originality in the bulk of the output, have wondered whether regeneration might not come from the national regions—in particular from Scotland and Wales. It is the same feeling—that the metropolis has in some areas fallen into cliché—which has made both critics and professionals in the business look hopefully to regional developments such as the setting-up of Yorkshire Television. In Scotland, commercial television has still to show that it is interested in pushing the claims of regional broadcasting into the area of serious, creative programming. On the face of it, the BBC should be in better case. Its new management is highly professional and enterprising. The direction it is able to take will, however, be determined by the National Broadcasting Council for Scotland, which shares with the Corporation responsibility for the policy and content of those programmes which are provided primarily for reception in Scotland. To quote the terms of the BBC's Charter, its functions are to be exercised with full regard to the distinctive culture, language, interests and tastes of the population of the country for which the Council is established. But like the other Councils and advisory bodies of the BBC, the National Broadcasting Council is, almost by definition, not likely to be a radical body. Its members, drawn from the ranks of that small circle of *bien-pensants* who, masquerading as 'housewives' or 'primary schoolteachers', appear on the lists of both ITA and BBC, will be for safety and not adventure. They are in a powerful position since, even before the date when the Council took over responsibility for programmes, the management of the BBC in Scotland had placed itself in a situation such as the Corporation as a whole has only reached with the recent assertion of the powers of the Chairman and Governors. At a period when the BBC as a whole is showing signs of caution and a turning away from radicalism in the programme field, it is not likely that the Scottish BBC—even under its vigorous new Controller—will blaze any trails. It can, of course, be argued that such conservatism is consonant with the mood of the country, that Scotland is not intellectually radical, that—to put it in terms of fashion—what goes in London will certainly not go in Edinburgh, that there is, in short, a cultural and social time-lag between North and South. It will require a radicalisation of Scottish life in all areas if Scottish television is to develop as a strong individual force serving Scotland and British television alike. Yet there must be some other more significant manifestation of Scottish life for television to offer its viewers at a peak viewing time on a Saturday evening than that mixture of sentimentality, militarism and bogus history—the Edinburgh Tattoo.